ENDORSEMENTS

"Daunted by many questions, Matthew J. Distefano needed to find the answers that would finally bring him the one thing he desired most—peace. However, the upcoming unveiling of the answers would only lead to more questions which, at times, would leave him questioning the very thing he had built his entire faith around—God. Here's a fantastic real-life story of one man's deconstruction and reconstruction to peace.

Enter Michelle Collins, who herself was once extremely challenged by a phrase Matthew once said, but is now helping him describe his journey. Michelle carefully and skillfully questions Matthew about his remarkable experience, while also adding valuable analysis and understanding to why he needed such a journey.

Matthew, who, like many people, grew up in or was at one point indoctrinated and influenced by the gripping vise of religious buffoonery, offers up a lively, honest, and real-life reflection of one man's process of how he questioned himself to freedom."

—Kyle Butler, Inspirational Motivator

"I've said there's only one way to deconstruct, and that's your way! In this very readable format of a conversation with Michelle Collins, we discover Matthew's way of deconstructing that will give others validation and encouragement for their own unique deconstruction journeys."

—**David Hayward, aka NakedPastor**

"Collins and Distefano have come together to offer an invitation into some of their most vulnerable and real moments in their deconstruction process. The reader is offered a front-row seat as they talk about their illuminating theological explorations that preceded their faith transitions. But more than sharing the ins and outs of their journeys, they intelligently and thoughtfully pursue what deconstruction looks like spiritually and psychologically, shedding further light on what something like this means for all areas of our lives. There is power in sharing your story. It allows others to be seen and know they are not alone and it releases something into the world that says, 'I have lived to tell.' This book is a must read for anyone engaging burning questions and curiosities of faith that beckon them toward new horizons. Collins and Distefano give strength for the journey ahead, while graciously and frankly reflecting on all the key moments that lead them toward freedom, liberation, and, of course, deconstruction."

—**Maria Francesca French, columnist for Patheos**

"Matthew's story is a raw, brutally honest journey that is all-too-familiar to many. His transparency has given a voice to those who still suffer in silence as they struggle to know a loving God who looks so very different than the one that they were exposed to in church. Thank you, Matthew and Michelle!"

—Romell D. Parks-Weekly, M.Div., Founding Pastor, The Sanctuary, St. Louis, MO

"*Learning to Float* is a helpful conversation between folks who have 'been there,' and although they are both experts in their field, they aren't hoping to provide 'how tos,' but to provide a sense of companionship on the journey of finding your own way. Deconstruction (as faith shifts seem to be referred to as lately) takes on many forms, but often leaves those who have experienced it feeling isolated and longing for community. This book provides the story of one person's journey and a sense that you are not alone in the process of renegotiating your relationship to your faith or the church. It's a great read!"

—Sarah Heath, ordained United Methodist Elder, author of *What's Your Story? Seeing Your Life Through God's Eyes*, and host of the Making Spaces podcast

"Many of us are discovering a tragic truth that much of Christianity doesn't look like Jesus. In fact, studies show that Christians are most known not for loving our neighbors, as Jesus commanded, but for being against certain neighbors. The Christian betrayal of Christ has led many to leave the faith altogether, but there are others who are deconstructing toxic Christianity we've been given. At the same time, we are looking for people to help us not just deconstruct, but also reconstruct a more Christlike faith. We need guides to help us. Fortunately, we have excellent guides in Michelle and Matthew."

—**Adam Ericksen, Education Director at The Raven Foundation**

"In *Learning to Float*, Matthew and Michelle are beautifully pastoral, exceptionally wise, and they write as fellow journeyers as opposed to know-it-all experts. Their inspiring friendship and down-to-earth communication styles birth a grace-filled dialogical literary delight that will help comfort and compassionately challenge any religious wanderer craving for a valuable resource as they travel through their deconstruction journey."

—**Mark Karris, author of *Religious Refugees: Deconstructing Toward Spiritual and Emotional Healing***

LEARNING TO FLOAT

Deconstructing Doctrinal Certainty
to Embrace the Mystery of Faith

MATTHEW J. DISTEFANO
with MICHELLE COLLINS

Copyright © 2022 by Matthew J. Distefano and Michelle Collins

First Edition

Cover design by Rafael Polendo (polendo.net)
Cover Illustration by Audrey Plis (shutterstock.com)
Layout by Matthew J. Distefano

Scripture quotations, unless otherwise noted, taken from the *New Revised Standard Version* and are copyright © 1989 by the Division of Christian Education of the National Council of Churches of Christ in the U.S.A. and are used by permission.

ISBN: 978-1-957007-20-5

This volume is printed on acid free paper and meets ANSI Z39.48 standards.
Printed in the United States of America

Published by Quoir
Oak Glen, California
www.quoir.com

DISCLAIMER

Disclaimer: The discussions contained herein were recorded and transcribed in 2021 and are *not* between a licensed therapist and her patient. Although Michelle Collins is working on her Psychology Doctorate, the authors want the reader to understand that these conversations are not a substitute for professional clinical therapy, diagnosis, or treatment, and are for informational purposes only.

DEDICATION

Dedicated to everyone who has experienced the pain of spiritual deconstruction

CONTENTS

FOREWORD

By Lindsey Paris-Lopez

When I was five, I tried to walk on water.

It was a chilly fall afternoon, and I was with my loving atheist father in the middle of a beautiful park. There were stones crossing a pond, and I had used them before to make my way to the other side.

But that day, I wanted to prove the existence of God to myself as much as to my father. It was more desperation and desire than "child-like faith" that made me seek to follow quite literally in Jesus' footsteps. And of course, it didn't work. Before I knew it, I was thrashing around in the water.

My father saved me, but I couldn't save his faith. And my own faith would be swept up in waves of questions and confusions and even existential dread for years to come.

Years later, I found myself standing at the edge of the James River. It was the beginning of the confirmation process into my church, and the story of Jacob wrestling with the angel of the Lord in the Jabbok was the guiding theme. I used the stones to cross the metaphorical Jabbok that time; my church eschewed Biblical literalism and welcomed questions and doubts. But even as I stayed above the literal waves, conflicting emotions were whipping up a storm within my soul.

The metaphor of wrestling with God in a river was both apt and terrifying to me. My whole life had been a battle to keep my head above water as I struggled to reconcile the loving God my church professed with the violent God of the Bible. The juxtaposition of steadfast love and mercy with a genocidal, geocidal deity who died to give us eternal life but would dole out eternal punishment if we couldn't wrap our minds and hearts around all the contradictions . . . I found myself nearly drowning in the whirlpool of confusion time and again.

I questioned my belief and even my desire to believe in such a God at all, especially when doing so felt like disloyalty to my father; and yet I still longed for the belonging and security I hoped would come with faith. Even as the idea of a God who wrestled and put hips out of joint in order to bless reinforced my fears and confusion, I had to admit I was wrestling with *something*.

There were islands of respite—safe harbors of friendships in which I could explore at least some of my questions. Gradually—through studying scripture and theology but much more through the love of family and friends—my perspective shifted. I began to see Scripture not as the univocal "Word of God," but as the story of Love breaking through human misunderstandings about God.

As fears slowly melted away, hope—not certainty, but deep, warm, comforting hope—broke through. My father's atheism, the different religious perspectives of the friends I made along the journey, and all the questions that came through these sources and so many others, were no longer sources of salvation-anxiety but expressions of Love in different languages that I could finally understand, if not speak fluently. And I finally came to a place where I could place my trust in unconditional, universal, redemptive Love.

But even as anxieties subsided into peace, new questions continually arose. Even when I thought I had finally crossed the Jabbok, new currents swept me back in. I finally began to realize that my faith journey would have no final destination this side of eternity. Because a faith journey is not just about beliefs, but about living a life of integrity and vulnerability and courage. And that journey looks different for everyone, but in every case, it encompasses the totality of who you are.

There are new twists and bends in the river—of faith, life, discovery, *everything*—with world events shifting the course from the outside and the Spirit navigating us from within. Sometimes the river is placid and sometimes it's turbulent. Sometimes we will have to swim, or even wrestle to keep our heads above water. But mostly, we have to learn how to live in the currents, to rest in the uncertainty and mystery. We have to learn to float.

That's where this book comes in.

This book is a life preserver when you find yourself adrift in the midst of your faith journey. When waves of doubt and anxiety threaten to rise above your head, or when you simply find yourself weary of swimming in the midst of unending waters, this book is your buoy. It's the gentle arms of friends holding you up so that you can breathe, even as currents of questions continue to sweep you up and move you along. It's the comforting whisper in your ear when you need it the most: "It's okay; I've got you. You're not alone."

Matthew Distefano knows his theology and philosophy, but far more importantly, he is 100-percent authentic. And as he mediates his story through conversation with Michelle Collins—whose wisdom, compassion, and friendship guide him as he articulates his deconstruction process—readers are bound to see parallels to their own journeys and struggles. I, for one, was grateful to see someone else whose questions and anxieties began as early as my own did. And the comfortable rapport between these close friends not only reminds me of the friendships that have been instrumental on my own journey, but also models the trust and vulnerability so necessary for breaking through anxiety.

This book is a reminder that there are people out there who can listen to our questions and doubts without judgment. Even when we feel most isolated and afraid, we are never alone. But at the same time, our journeys are unique, running parallel and intersecting at times but never converging entirely. That's why this is not a how-to guide, but a literary companion, a friend and a source of comfort by two friends who model how to comfort and support one another.

Even as your struggles and questions and anxieties take unique form as they are filtered through your life and experiences, they resonate with those of others. There are common denominators throughout most faith journeys as well as differentiating factors. How does a culture steeped in exclusive and violent interpretations of Christianity (regardless of what is said by our individual churches, if we even attend them) influence how we understand God? How does our relationship with our families shape us in early childhood and onward? What about the contradictory messages about sex and sexuality thrown at us from different directions from our churches and the broader culture? Matthew guides us through all of these twists and stages of his journey and then some, highlighting their significance and sharing the wisdom he has gleaned. Michelle's intuitive questions and connections open pathways to deep insights and model the way friendly conversation can bring us to new discoveries and deep truths.

Listening to Matthew's story and seeing how it resonates with Michelle, even as it differs from her own, helps to ease the doubts we all sometimes have, the nagging lies telling us that no one could possibly understand us. And just knowing that can be motivation enough to keep going, to not let the waters overtake us.

The most wonderful thing about this book is that it demonstrates that beyond the anxieties that so often accompany our deconstruction processes, there is hope, humor, and joy. When we realize we are not alone, that we can share and laugh and cry and wonder together, we find new dimensions that we never would have seen if we had stayed wherever it was that we came from before. That doesn't mean everyone will leave their churches or environments behind, but it does mean our minds will continually open to new ways of understanding who we are and who we are becoming.

I now interpret Jesus' walking on water not so much as a miracle, but as the ability to navigate a chaotic and turbulent world with grace and integrity. Whatever you may believe about the historicity of that story, it can serve to teach us to embrace the fluidity of a world in transition. The certainties and solid surfaces on which we may rest for a time can wash away, but that need not overwhelm us.

"Learning to float" is the perfect metaphor for not only surviving, but soaking in the beauty of our faith journeys as we recognize that they never truly end. So lay back and enjoy the ride.

PREFACE

By Matthew J. Distefano

Jesus loves me, this I know, for the Bible tells me so.

Are you sure? What happens if you don't love him back?

I'm good. I go to Church. I read my Bible (sometimes). I got baptized.

But you also watched porn today. And yesterday. And the day before that.

Yeah, but every Christian's a sinner. I'm fine. I've gotta stop stressing about it.

Or, maybe you're exactly the type of Christian who gets left behind.

I won't be. The Bible tells me so . . .

The Bible tells you a lot of things. Do you really wanna know what else it says?

~~~~~~~~~~~

Have you had internal conversations like these? If you're a Christian, or have ever been a Christian, I'm guessing you have. Maybe not all the time, and especially not during those summer retreats in the woods, when Jesus-induced endorphins flowed though you at break-neck speeds, but in your quietest moments, with the lights turned off and your head firmly planted in your pillow, I'm sure your mind has wandered into places deeper and darker than even the Mines of Moria.

For me, the deepest and darkest place was called hell. More specifi-cally, eternal conscious torment. Even as a youngster—say, maybe age five or six—I understood that an eternal hell was where we all went when we died—unless, of course, we signed up for Team Jesus™. Nothing was assured, however. Looming in the back of any Christian's mind, no matter one's age, are those passages that remind us how we are never truly safe. The one that stuck out to me the most came from Matthew 7. You probably know the passage: "Not everyone who says to me, 'Lord, Lord,' will enter the kingdom of heaven . . . On that day many will say to me, 'Lord, Lord, did we not prophesy in your name, and cast out demons in your name, and do many deeds of power in your name?' Then I will declare to them, 'I never knew you; go away from me, you evildoers.'" (Matthew' 7:21–23) I. Never. Knew. You. Four words that haunted me from the moment I heard them boldly and proudly trumpeted from the pulpit. Every time I did evil—whether I cussed under my breath, found myself at that same adult website again, refused to help the homeless man on the corner, or even skipped out on yet another Bible study—this passage would come knocking on my mind's door. And yet, it did nothing to push me toward righteousness and away from sin. In fact, it did the opposite.

That's the thing about fear and shame. Neither ever really act as the motivator we hope them to be. I'm living proof of that. I tried, and I tried, and I tried some more to diligently read my Bible, to forget those naughty URLs that beckoned me daily, to clean up my foul language, and to treat everyone how I would want to be treated, but I failed. Hard. Why? Because fear only gets you so far. It only motivates you so much. And then it leaves you paralyzed. Cold. Ashamed. Numb. Wanting to do better, yet frozen; wanting to be a light in the world, yet going nowhere but under the covers of your twin-sized bed.

For me, this struggle went on for years, decades even. And while it may not have been a minute-by-minute battle, it was always with me in some way. Like it was for Sméagol, Gollum was always there, lurking in the shadows. Even when I made progress, when I would rid myself of even a tiny dose of fear and shame, they were still there. Watching. Waiting. Biding their time. Knowing that at some point, my defenses would come down. Then they would strike and I would recoil into the deep places of my tormented mind, which of course only made things worse. Cyclically, I would spiral. Fear. Shame. Paralysis. Rinse. Wash. Repeat.

All the while, my anger built. Anger towards myself, no doubt. But also anger toward the God who made me this way. Why did I have to be so fucked-up? Why didn't my friends seem to have the same fears? Why did I feel so alone when Christian community was supposed to be a salve for healing? Why did I have so many goddamn questions? Questions and yet no answers—none that satisfied, anyway.

And then there were the questions about God's nature. Why was his solution to my sin so archaic? Hell? Wrath? Eternal torment? Violence to the nth degree? Abandonment times a trillion? I had a dad who left me when I was at my most vulnerable so why did I need a heavenly father who was exactly the same? He is the one who made me, right? Then why was he going to hold my ineptitude against me for all eternity? Again, so many questions, yet so few answers.

Then it happened: I walked away. I could no longer worship this God, so what was the point in even believing he was there? It was all too much to bear, so I bailed. I bailed on my church. I bailed on my faith. I bailed on . . . *everything*, really. Well, not everything. I still did my best to be a good person. I still did my best to love my friends and family. I just did it without the religious jargon and need to prove myself to some tyrant in the sky. And even though it wasn't the most comfortable thing in the world—a 180-degree turn rarely is—it was better than the alternative. It was better than knowing some deity who seemed no better than me would be judging me some day. At least I could rest a little in my fucked-up-ness.

What I didn't realize, however, was that this resting place would only be temporary. It was respite from the desert, sure, but there was still travelling to do. I was in Rivendell but home was Hobbiton—in the Shire, up on Bagshot Row. But how I got there exactly will have to wait until I talk with my good friend Michelle, if for no other reason than she is the best Sherpa that I can think of. And while she is currently working on her psychology doctorate, don't think of these conversations as a substitute for the counseling I have desperately needed. Instead, they are simply a discussion—about faith, about life, about losing everything in order to find it again. And they are conversations between longtime friends and trusted confidants. Nothing more and nothing less. But in the midst of the desert, in the midst of the road to Mordor and back, oftentimes all you need is a trusted partner and loyal friend. Michelle is one of these, and I'm certain as you read this book, you'll find yourself agreeing with me.

MATTHEW'S ACKNOWLEDGMENTS

I would like to start by thanking my wife Lyndsay for all of her support throughout the years. I'm constantly impressed with her strength, vulnerability, and willingness to grow.

Our daughter Elyse has made me a better man. I've learned a lot from her even though she is still a child.

I can't begin to express how much gratitude I have for my best friend Michael Machuga. Not only has he been an excellent coauthor and cohost of our Bonfire Sessions podcast, but he has been a trusted confidant for nearly a decade.

Speaking of trusted confidant: Michelle Collins. Thank you so much, my friend . . . for everything. It's been a joy writing this book with you.

To the members of the Heretic Happy Hour podcast: Thank you. Everyone involved with the show are some of the best people I know.

My parents Dave and Sharon Wohnoutka have been super supportive, and so I would like to mention them both here.

A hearty "thank you" to everyone who supports me on Patreon.

And finally, thanks to everyone I don't have the space to mention by name. I have many friends, supporters, readers, listeners, and sounding boards, and I am grateful for each and every one of you.

MICHELLE'S ACKNOWLEDGMENTS

Acknowledgements are difficult for me as there are always so many people that you feel you should include and yet that is of course not possible. I do want to acknowledge my family's patience and support while I wandered aimlessly in the wilderness, trying to understand what was happening. My ongoing angst and anger with God and the organized church specifically were often the topic of conversation and I assume they tired of it as often as I did. There were those fellow sojourners along the way that helped cushion the blow of rejection and depression that came along for the journey. Several that spring to mind are Rudy Zacharias, Rob Martin, Jeff Robinson, and Carol Wimmer—thanks to each of you for being vulnerable in your journey and always willing to indulge a rant or some tears with understanding. While we have only met sparingly, I am reminded often through your posts of your incredible depth of love and comradery for those that are traveling the same road.

The topic of deconstruction is often at the expense of those who work diligently within the four walls of the church. Pastors often get lumped into the vortex of those experiencing this emotional disarray. While some deserve anger, far more are those who labor quietly with love and provide a soft-landing place to those of us who need that comfort. Specifically, for me are the aforementioned Rob Martin, Mike and Marilyn Miller, and Paul Bergmann. I know that each of you has dealt with your own questions, disappointments, challenges, as well as some trauma along the way. I applaud you for still striving to look like Jesus and pulling it off so very well. Additionally, thank you for always being such a wonderful example of love and care for your fellow human beings. I want to be like each of you when I grow up!

There are several that have provided huge amounts of support and love along the way, and I want to be sure to thank you specifically. To one of my dearest friends, Matthew Distefano, thank you for always being a phone call away and for being an amazing friend even when I am horrible at communication or not able to bring myself to reach out. You always do! I love you! In that same vein, Seth Showalter, thank you for being a steadfast and important voice in my life. You have indulged my emotions even when I am positive you had no idea what to say and for that I value you as a great friend. I love you!

Finally, thank you to those very special friends I have made in the last year who have come alongside me personally when my whole world turned upside down. Sharon Boykin, thank you for showing me that I can continue on and that I am stronger than I believe.

INTRODUCTION

By Michelle Collins

As with most things, I am not quite sure how to begin this discussion. Not because I don't have experience with the process but because the process is so large and so subjective that finding a place to enter the conversation is daunting. But I suppose I can begin with my relationship to Matthew. First and foremost, I will say he is one of my closest friends and, as he stated in the preface, a trusted confidant. When our relationship began, it was nothing more than one of hundreds of Facebook relationships that I enjoyed. I am unsure of how we became friends but nevertheless, we were. Matthew had just finished his book *All Set Free* and was promoting it. Based on his posts and the subject matter of his book, I found myself intrigued and interested in what he was sharing. It sounded a lot like something I was experiencing. I had been removed from my church, I was reading and investigating all I could find on different tenets within Christianity, and I was truly seeking answers. I had lost my face-to-face community and was leaning more and more on those with whom I found something in common on social media.

As someone who has always gone out of my way to encourage and support my friends in their endeavors, I found myself agreeing to a long-ass drive to meet with people I had never met in order to show my support for Matthew and his new book. I am often deeply thankful that I did so. I found even more people with whom I had a connection but most importantly, I got to know Matthew and understand where his heart was as it pertained to God. He was not afraid to share his discomfort with God and all things Christian. I would later find that this openness was not something he shared with many at that time.

We now have a name for the process of questioning that many were starting to vocalize. It has become known as deconstruction, and brings with it a lot of emotional baggage. Depending upon the person and the experiences that lead to their deconstruction, we can find joy and happiness, pain and anger, or even sadness and depression. In all reality, someone should write a book about the emotional and psychological toll this process has on a person . . . oh wait, that's right, I did write that book. Okay, enough shameless self-promotion . . . Matthew seemed to be ahead of me in this journey of exploration (if we could identify a linear timeline) and as such, I learned to lean on him for support and asked him questions that seemed out of my reach. I still give him credit for my stay in agnosticism and atheism. I know that sounds bad, but what I mean is that he told me a day would come that I would question the existence of God. At the time, I did not believe him. Further, when I did reach that place, it was his sage voice that told me the only way out of this process was to go through the process. I think I hated him a little for saying that, but I have found that he was oh-so-right. I have survived the process thus far and can honestly say that every now and then I can see the light at the end of the tunnel.

So, what then is the purpose of this writing? Within the last few years, I have found myself back in school studying a subject that is far outside my areas of expertise; yet something keeps beckoning me forward in the study of psychology. Maybe it is because everything in life emotionally and psychologically affects us on some level, but more so, the number of people experiencing this saga that has become known as deconstruction continues to grow, as does the need to understand it. I speak with people that are at all levels of this journey and the overarching theme that continues to show up is how emotionally tasking it all is.

Matthew recently approached me about writing down his trek through deconstruction, the tenets of Christianity that seemed most problematic for him, as well as the fears and emotions that went with him on the journey. His idea was to treat it as a counseling experience, to allow you, the reader, to be privy to his emotions, his questions, his thoughts, and his conclusions in a setting that mirrors that of a case study in psychology. What we found, however, is that rather than a counseling session, this became more of a conversation in which we both contributed our experiences. It is at this point that I feel I must again reiterate that I am not a licensed counselor or therapist. I am merely a student at this point; I am also a certified life coach who is living this process in my own unique way. So, while I was going to present this in a case study format, instead I will attempt to describe some of the psychological implications that I see in Matthew's experience (and quite honestly in most experiences that have been shared with me from those who identify in a deconstructive process) and then we can begin a conversation that allows for open and free dialogue into the realms of the emotional reality of deconstruction. Please note: this is my interpretation of the psychological implications, but this should in no way be taken as an official diagnosis. Instead, it is a starting point for those strong points of contention that seem most evident.

Common Psychological Implications

Most people who self-identify with the subject and experience of deconstruction seem to have common struggles with some emotional and psychological issues. In the course of our conversation, Matthew's descriptions seem consistent with symptoms of post-traumatic stress syndrome, obsessive-compulsive tendencies, and generalized anxiety disorder. As a child and into adulthood, Matthew was surrounded by those with whom he shared a religious belief system. Further, continued expectations of "good" behavior, as defined by those within his church, set the stage for a continual cycle of "sin and repentance." The ideas of a violent God and supposed retribution or eternal consequences for his actions served to reinforce his own thoughts of not being good enough, constant worry of failure, the possibility of lost community, and excommunication from God if he were unable to behave in a manner sufficient to the belief system and those with whom he interacted personally. Constantly exposed to ideas of a violent God, Matthew became hypervigilant about his perceived safety and that of his family, as well as fears of being "left behind" if God were to suddenly and without warning remove those who had believed well enough.

Post-Traumatic Stress Syndrome

While events such as accidents, fires, or the death of a loved one can produce post-traumatic stress syndrome (PTSD), violence seems to be the largest catalyst. As many within Christianity can attest, the teaching of God's wrath as a catalyst for hell, as well as the violent and frightening end times eschatology, leads to a constant worry for one's safety and the well-being of loved ones. As Matthew was living in an environment that feared and revered a violent God-construct, the daily fear of not measuring up, thus resulting in God's wrath, served as almost constant exposure to a violent mindset. Further, the acceptance of this idea from family and close friends served to disallow honest dialogue, including questions. Rather, rote acceptance of these violent ideals created an atmosphere that served to set up an ongoing emotional reaction at specific Christian triggers. While most people deal with stress and anxiety in ways that are healthier, those who experience traumatic events, and especially those events that are repeated, tend to become less able to work through the trauma in a healthy fashion. "PTSD is frequently comorbid with other disorders such as depression, substance abuse, and anxiety disorders such as obsessive-compulsive disorder, panic disorder, agoraphobia, and social anxiety."[1]

Obsessive-Compulsive Disorder

I want to be careful when discussing this disorder with regards to deconstruction. In general, obsessive-compulsive disorder (OCD) presents as an uncontrollable urge or thought that results in compulsive behavior in order to cope with the anxiety produced. Obsessive ideation is experienced as unwelcome and unwanted thoughts that are often ignored until they become overwhelming. While many who struggle with this disorder do so as a way in which to control their surroundings, in an effort to reduce generalized anxiety, those within religious deconstruction seem to approach this as a way to appease God, thereby lowing or controlling their anxiety. While there are multiple associated features surrounding OCD, fears of harm to either oneself or loved ones produces a "checking" compulsion.[2]

Per Matthew's descriptions, his early childhood and young adulthood were spent in an atmosphere of perceived religious dissatisfaction, resulting in fears of losing his family and being disowned by God. As such, he is predisposed to thoughts of safety and well-being and avoiding "hell" at all costs. While Matthew has described his behavior as damaging in hindsight, during his deconstruction, those thoughts and fears did sometimes return and, once again, he was left struggling with rote behaviors like Bible reading, prayer, and other obsessive behavior that would seem to placate an angry deity. Those events triggering an OCD response can include, "a sense of incompleteness or uneasiness until things look, feel, or sound just right."[3] Hence, his surroundings seem incomplete without the hypervigilance associated with existential safety, which produces within him this sense of unease.

I have highlighted only several of the issues that many are experiencing as they deconstruct their beliefs. It is easy to dismiss the psychological implications of such an undertaking, but we would be remiss in doing so. Everything is psychological; it all matters on an emotional level. I do recognize that this all seems hyper dramatic; however, currently there is no allowance for religious abuse in the diagnostic manual, nor is there anything close the existential crisis that is happening for many people. The closest we can come is complex PTSD, which is denoted as regular PTSD situations that are experienced over and over. Religious abuse seems to happen every week as we are exposed to a violent God, stringent, unattainable standards, and a community that inflicts its own sense of justice when one steps out of line or questions the prevailing religious mindset. While much of what Matthew may discuss is outside of this exact diagnosis, these are the underlying issues that seem most evident to me in his descriptions, as well as from my own experience in this same religious mindset. Again, this is not a real therapy situation but rather a discussion among friends who trust one another and can show support and love in the process of better understanding this psychological journey. So, let's get started . . .

---

1. Ray, *Abnormal Psychology*, 266–67.

2. American Psychiatric Association, "Obsessive-Compulsive and Related Disorders," 239.

3. Ibid.

SETTING THE STAGE OF DECONSTRUCTION

Session One

Michelle Collins: Whenever we have conversations like the ones we are about to embark on, it's a good idea to have a goal: What is it that we're hoping to attain or to achieve in doing this project? Do we have a specific purpose in mind? While we recognize that this is a conversation, it is first and foremost your story, so *you* get to set the tone. It may, of course, include some of my own experiences, because after years of knowing you, I think they're somewhat similar. For the most part, however, this whole endeavor is about providing space for you to talk through what you need to talk about.

Matthew J. Distefano: While this is my story, it is actually a collaborative effort. So, my goal is to provide a resource for people so that when they find themselves deep in the throes of deconstruction, they will be able to—and I don't want to hijack the #MeToo movement—say "me too." My hope is that they'll say things like, "I've felt the same things these authors have as I've asked questions about my faith, as I've questioned my worldview, as I've questioned the things that I was told were true about the Universe." In other words, I want to be able to

1

provide a level of vulnerability that allows people to not feel a sense of extreme dread the minute they discover they don't know what's what any longer. In talking to faith-questioning people over the years, there seems to be a pattern. Everyone has a unique experience, of course, but there seems to be a pattern as to what happens when you start to, as Richard Rohr would put it, get into the second half of life.[1] And that can happen in your twenties, in your thirties, in your forties, or it may never happen. It's not necessarily about your age, but it's about getting to a place where you are kind of just floundering, questioning, lamenting, or shaking your fist at the sky. And I know you've gone through this and are continuing to go through this. I've also gone through it, so I want to tell my story, because while I think it's a unique and interesting story—maybe I'm narcissistic in saying that—it's also quite similar to other people's stories, too. And there's nothing better than being able to commiserate with others. There's nothing better than having people to connect with, especially as we deal with these deep, existential questions.

MC: Right. One of my contentions, of course, is that there are different levels of deconstruction. What I mean by that is some people just deconstruct a handful of the things they believe, like hell, or an infallible Bible, or things along those lines, but then there is a deeper level of deconstruction that happens where you begin to question your relationship to God or where you even fit into the grand scheme of things. Perhaps even further beyond that is the deconstruction of yourself as a human being, because so much of what we have believed in the past about God influences who we are as people. Christianity is very much into saying that our faith is our identity, so when you begin to deconstruct your Christianity, you tend to lose your identity. Some never reach that level of deconstruction, but many in fact do. Does that sound accurate to you? Do you feel as if you've traversed that spectrum a little further than most others have?

MJD: Based on my conversations with so many people over the years, I tend to think so. I know that some folks, from what I understand, are able to just "deconstruct" theoretical ideas. But, before we get too far along in the conversation, let's talk about that word "deconstruction." Although we are both familiar with Jacques Derrida (the French philosopher who coined the term), we're not primarily using it in the same way he did (we've deconstructed the word deconstruction, haven't we?). Instead, we're using it in the way most folks on social media do, where it essentially means to question or tear down that which you once believed in order to then reconstruct or build something else in its stead. People are able to do that, for the most part, with, like you said, eternal torment, or penal substitutionary atonement theory, or their scary-as-hell eschatology, or whatever the case may be—their belief about the Bible or theory of inspiration of the Scriptures—and kind of leave it at that. But, for me, it went all the way down to my identity—the core of who I am—because my identity was so tied up in my belief about what God was like. When I got to a place where I didn't even believe in God any longer, I was almost forced to ask questions like, "Well, what does it even mean to be *me*? What does it mean to be a human being without God?" Getting to these sorts of questions isn't bad because in most Christian circles you're taught that humans are wretched worms, so not having that toxicity hanging over you any longer is a good thing. It's certainly healthy, but you're also left without *any* sort of identity. So, I think what people need to understand is that there are "levels" to deconstruction, to put it loosely, and for many people, including myself, it goes well beyond the theological. It gets all the way into the relational, to places you

3

would never even think. It gets into sex. You deconstruct sex because, I mean, good God, the purity culture—especially for women but also for men, too—is so prevalent in Christianity. And it's so damn toxic. We have to be puritanical because if we have sex before marriage, we're tainted—again, this is especially true for women.

MC: Damaged goods.

MJD: Exactly. And so, you get to a place where you're deconstructing things that you would never have even originally thought. For a lot of people, they're kind of secondary. It starts with, "I can no longer believe in hell," or, "I can no longer believe in an inerrant Bible," because you became an adult and grew up, realizing that you can put away childish things now, but you typically don't stop there. In other words, while the process is different for everyone, if you keep exploring the rabbit trail, it does seem to get down all the way to, "Who am I?" You know, those really deep existential questions.

MC: Also, the further you go along in that process, the longer the process takes. And that is terrifying. I made mention recently that if I had thought at the beginning of this that I would be seven years into deconstruction, I think I would have had a mental breakdown because I couldn't imagine seven years of feeling uncertain and unclear about my identity. But, of course, I didn't feel those emotions all the way through. They came up as I went along. And it does start out with those little questions. To use an analogy, it reminds me of a little spring that bubbles up somewhere—just little drips of water—and then as it goes along it becomes this larger body of water. That's what this feels like. You start with these little, nagging questions, and as you begin to explore those it only leads to more questions, which only leads to more uncertainty, and before you know it, you're in this full-blown process that is somewhat demoralizing, somewhat unstable—or, actually, completely unstable—and then suddenly you're afloat in the middle of something that you don't know how to get out of. I don't know if that resonates with you but that was definitely my experience. It's actually still how I feel a lot of the times.

MJD: It does, and I don't even know how you necessarily get out of that. It just kind of happens and you become comfortable in the uncertainty.

MC: You learn to float.

MJD: You learn to float. Exactly! And it doesn't necessarily mean you've gone anywhere; you've just learned how to be comfortable in an otherwise uncomfortable environment. I think it's why I get into trouble sometimes. Certain people I'll come across will be in the early-questions stage—you know, it's just a trickle—but I've been floating for a while now, so will say things completely off-handed and flippant and that will just wreck the person.

MC: Which is what you did to me.

MJD: Honestly, I don't even remember. Remind me about when I did this.

MC: You told me there would come a time when I would question whether God existed or not, but of course I was only at a place where I was willing to question *my* brand of Christianity, whether or not it may have been correct or knowledgeable enough. In other words, maybe I didn't fully understand that there was something beyond penal substitutionary atonement or maybe there were other eschatological viewpoints I didn't know, but it never occurred to me that I would reach a point where I would question God's very existence. I've believed in God since I was a little girl. So, you said what you said, and I thought, "No, that won't happen to me." But then it did, and it rocked me pretty hard. It still does. The other day, my daughter asked me, "Do you believe in God?" And I said, "Today? Yes. But tomorrow it may be different." I've had to learn to be comfortable—well, somewhat comfortable—with that answer. But I remember when I came to you and said, "Yeah, I reached that spot. You told me I would. And I don't want to be here." Your comment to me was, "The only way out of this process is through." I have not forgotten that because you're right; there is no backing away from this process. We can try. We can put it on hold for a while. We can freeze in place. But eventually, our questions remain. They continue. And it's a part of life. It's a part of our evolution of thought, of being and identity, and all these things that we've been taught we're supposed to know right away in Christianity (but really don't).

MJD: Once you've peaked behind the veil, you can't unsee what you've seen.

MC: You mentioned Richard Rohr a little bit ago, and one of the things I've taken away from some of his writings is that the first part of your life is spent building a box, and the second part of your life is deciding what to put in that box. I've found that to be very apropos. We had a foundation, but then when we began to really think about it, or question it, now we're deciding which of those things actually makes sense in remaining a part of our reality. That's going to be different for every person. I do believe there's an objective truth, but I don't know that we get to know it now. That's my thought process, and so I think that it's erroneous to think that in order to be mentally healthy we have to have 100% trust in our identity. This whole game is about learning as we go along.

MJD: It's one of the paradoxes of the universe, I believe. There is an objective truth, and we can only approach it subjectively.

MC: Exactly.

MJD: Yet here we are. Good luck, right?

MC: Always exciting. It reminds me of that old story about a bunch of blind men who try to describe an elephant, and they all do it differently because as they do so, they're touching different parts of it. Maybe that's how this works. Maybe we don't get to see the whole elephant right now. Maybe that's later. But maybe that comes back to some of the stuff we'll be getting into as we go along. You know, what happens after all of this? What happens after death? That's a part of the pondering of a lot of people. And you have provided a number of bullet points that you thought were probably important in your process. It's easy to say, "Let's start at the beginning," as that may be a different place for each person, but do you want to start there now?

MJD: Yes. I think this has been a fine introduction for what we will be attempting to do in this book. Let's pick it back up in the next session and start from the proverbial beginning. Where did I come from spiritually and how did it go so wrong from there?

1. Rohr talks about the two halves of life in many places, but primarily in *Falling Upward: A Spirituality for the Two Halves of Life*: San Francisco: Jossey-Bass, 2011.

THE EARLY YEARS

Session Two

Michelle Collins: In the first session, we talked a little bit about what our ideas about deconstruction were. We introduced who we are and what the conversation is going to entail. So, now were ready to get more into the specifics of your experience, and there's no better place to start than the beginning. How early was it that you remember having any kind of relationship with God, or the idea or concept of God?

Matthew J. Distefano: I don't know if I have an exact date or age but I would say it was anywhere between five and seven. And I say that because I *do* remember being baptized when I was nine. So, I knew that it was important for me to—and I say this with my tongue firmly planted in my cheek—"give my heart to the Lord" at a fairly early age, before the age of accountability, as it were. But I didn't really know what any of that really meant; I just knew that Jesus was important in some way. The problem was that there was always this element of fear behind it all, because along with my belief in Jesus came the belief in hell. Along with my belief in Jesus, there was the belief in the End Times, the Rapture, the *Left Behind* theology of Hagee and Lindsey and all those blowhards. And so, there wasn't a single instance where

I remember believing in Jesus without an attachment to some really scary scenario at the end of days, whenever the end was—during this life, maybe, we didn't know when the rapture was going to take place. But, if not in this life, certainly when we died there was to be this great ultimatum. My beliefs were always attached to that, from even as early as five, but perhaps as late as seven. Either way, I was pretty damn young to be wrestling with this type of shit.

MC: Even that early, you were introduced to topics like rapture theory and hell? You didn't get the feel-good Jesus? You know, the *Jesus loves me, this I know* Jesus?

MJD: I got that as well but there was always a footnote. I got the *Jesus loves me, this I know* Jesus, but the things that really stuck out to me and sort of attached themselves to my brain were the passages that were more threatening—you know, the "Lord, Lord" one, as well as the one about the unpardonable sin. I would always think, quite literally (as any child would), "Have I done that? And if it's unpardonable, what's the point of life now?"

MC: That's not just a kid-thing, though. Even as adults—I wasn't introduced to that topic as a child, but as I got older, I came across it—immediately my first thought was, "Oh my gosh, have I done the unpardonable sin?" Every Christian has wondered that at some point or another. It's pretty unusual, though, to think about that as a young child.

MJD: After talking with so many folks over the years, I have found that to be the case. And the thing is, my parents weren't hardcore fire-and-brimstone Christians; it was more the churches we went to.

My parents—and I wouldn't call them liberal—but they weren't pick-eting or street preaching or anything like that. You know, my stepdad was a hippie at one point in his life and both he and my mom were raised Catholic and then became Protestants, so they had both gone through some sort of transformation. And I feel like when you do that, you're not as hardcore. (Plus, both had gone through a divorce before getting remarried, so "judge not, lest ye be judged," and all that.) But maybe that's just my experience. Regardless, I remember that particular passage; I also remember the passage where Jesus warns about calling people a "fool," or "raca," and that one was big because I called my brothers worse things than that. So, I must have been in danger of hellfire, as the Scriptures put it. And then of course the "Lord, Lord," one—that one really got me. You know the one: "There will be those who say to me 'Lord, Lord,' and I will say to them, 'I never knew you.'" I always thought how harsh and terrible that sounded, and I was scared to death the entire time.

MC: Especially as a kid. That's really scary because I'm sure that every time you screwed up, that passage would play in the back of your head. But very rarely does anyone follow that up with any kind of explanation or assurance. At least in my experience, my parents and grandparents were very much okay with fear being a motivator. As opposed to allaying those fears, they were much more inclined to say, "Well, that's just how it works, so we've got to be good . . . or else." That kind of thinking can be very damaging.

MJD: It was. And so, I tried to do the things that would assure my salvation. So, for instance, I would try to read my Bible, but it was just so damn confusing. I would try to be motivated to go to church, but it was so often boring. I would try to join Bible studies when I was in my teen years, but it was probably just because there were cute girls there. And look, I did all the things that good Christians are supposed to do, but the reality is that fear doesn't motivate us as much as we'd like to think it does. It can motivate us for a while because it scares the hell out of us and we do what we need to do, but that well runs dry pretty quickly.

MC: It's a defeated motivation. Like you said, after a while, if you're afraid that you've already done the unpardonable, what the hell, live how you're gonna live then because you've already done the damage.

MJD: Nihilism for the win, right?

MC: Absolutely. You made mention of your family just a moment ago, and you even mentioned a stepdad, so what was the family dynamic when you were young?

MJD: To be honest, it was a bit of a bumpy ride. My mom and bio-dad—I now refer to him simply as a sperm donor—divorced when I was five, so that would have been in '87. My mom quickly remarried a man who then became my stepdad, and they had a bit of a tumultuous go of it. There was a separation, maybe two—I can't quite remember. We moved back and forth between my house in Santa Cruz, California and my grandparents' house in San Jose because of their rocky relationship during the first couple years of marriage. But my relationship with my father, specifically, was one of those that I wanted to happen really badly but just never did. And so, around age 12, I just sort of threw up my hands and said, "Fuck it, I'm not going to keep pursuing this any longer," because he made it abundantly clear that, in spite of his words to the contrary, he was not interested. Now, of course, I do believe there is a theological point to be made with that. And I say that because if we're going to talk about God as "father," it certainly raises the question: What kind of father? If you have had an experience like mine—a father who was absent, who was quite punitive, who could be a nice guy at times but very apathetic other times, who was very good at projecting his own insecurities onto others, who eventually blamed my attitude for us not having a relationship—but then you're also supposed to view God as father, you're kinda left wondering what that really means.

MC: That brings up a good point, and that was actually one of the things I was going to ask you: there is the idea out there that is pretty prevalent, which is that your idea of God and your relationship to God is often dependent upon what your relationship with your earthly father looks like. I was always inclined to ask, even from a very young age, "What if you had a shitty father?" And look, I don't like to say that about my dad because I *do* have a relationship with him now, but he wasn't there when I was a kid . . . ever. I didn't feel like he loved me, so it often made me question if God is like that, how do I know God really loves me? Do you think that colored your viewpoint of God at an early age?

MJD: I would say it did, but the silver-lining was my stepdad was a good dad, and my grandfather (who recently passed away) was great—a true, noble father-figure to the nth degree. So, I experienced a spectrum as a kid and it caused a split; that is, maybe God's like my father or maybe God's like my grandfather. When I started to get older, then—when I started to think more critically, more rationally—I started to weigh these issues and then realized the things we're saying about God are aligning more with the dad I have had a negative experience with. So, we could wax poetic that God is love and all these other nice ideas but if you have hell, if you have wrath, if you have anger, if you have punitive justice, if you have retribution, if you have violence—you know, qualities that looked more similar to my biological dad than my loving grandfather—and you're asking me to worship *this* God, that's where I had, and continue to have, a hard time. If I had to put my finger on why I started deconstructing, then, that's definitely a part of it. Simply put: God wasn't nearly as "good" as my grandfather, and that was a problem.

MC: That definitely seems to cause a break somewhere in the matrix, so to speak. I've had those same thoughts about God. I couldn't reconcile a loving God, even though that's what I was constantly told. But in my experience, and I don't know about you, there was so much disharmony evident in my life, and people used that disharmony in a very punitive way, but would then say, "I love you." So, my ideas of love were pretty warped anyway. Then, to say that God loves you, it became much easier to see God as this vindictive, wrathful person and still associate that with "God is love." Honestly, that's what it looked like around me, as fucked-up as that is. I think the point that I hear in what you're saying is this: as a kid, it's really hard to discern what God is supposed to look like and—you mentioned your grandfather, stepfather, and biological father—is he somewhere, on any given day, on the spectrum of where those people are? Or, is God constant? And I don't know if a kid thinks these things but maybe asks, "Is God angry? Is God supposed to love me? Is God supposed to accept me? Am I going to hell?" Questions like these.

MJD: But you see, my grandfather was not really on a broad spectrum. He was constant. And yeah, as a kid I wasn't thinking, "Well, the nature of God seems rather Janus-faced . . . yada, yada, yada." I wasn't thinking those things. It was pure rawness. It was thoughts like, "How could there be a hell?" or, "You're God; do something!" You know, the types of rhetorical questions folks ask. And then, a big part of all this for me was that my grandfather, who was *the* constant in my life—my grandmother, of course, was also a constant, so I can't forget to mention her—wasn't a Christian. That's something that really rocked me. He was the most loving man I knew. He was the kindest man I knew. Any time we had a problem he opened his home to us. And yet, I guess hell awaited him because he hadn't given his heart to the Lord. Even as a kid, I would think, "How dare you! God, how dare you!" My father, who was a Christian, a born-again Evangelical, was good to go. But my grandfather wasn't. This, I could never reconcile.

MC: So, we have a conundrum: How do we view salvation? How do we view people and the way they treat us in life? Are we supposed to rely on the fact that good people are saved and bad people aren't, while the evidence is in our face that supports otherwise? Or, do we get to the point, even as kids, where we recognize that all people are fallible? I don't know, but I do know this: kids are pretty blunt and fairly honest in their questioning, especially when it comes to what they think is right and wrong. So, you were onto something; you could look at hell and say, "that's not fair," especially when it came to someone like your grandfather. Let me ask you, was he your mom's dad?

MJD: Yeah.

MC: Okay, that's what I would have thought because it seems like he wouldn't have allowed his son to act the way he did toward you.

MJD: Definitely not. And my grandmother certainly would not have. She was a spicy Sicilian woman and she would have been on his ass with a marinara-soaked spatula.

MC: Do you think there was anything in your father's past that accounted for the way he was?

MJD: Absolutely. And that's the thing! Recognizing this is a part of growing up and what allows me to step back and offer forgiveness to him. It doesn't change anything for him and frankly, he doesn't even know that I've forgiven him. It's just in my own heart where this has occurred. Let me give you an example. His mother, for instance, never told him who his dad was and from what I understand refused to tell him anything about the man (it turns out that based on my personal genetics, he may have been a Turkish/Iranian fellow, and also a one-night stand). So, when I learned *that*, it really put things into perspective. This dude is obviously sub or non-consciously passing on the trauma he's experienced. We know this through brain science, through psychology—there is intergenerational trauma that we can pass on. I saw it in the group homes when I did social work. I saw the pattern, and it forces you, not to excuse anyone's behavior, but to put things into perspective. You can say, "Okay, he was quite fucked-up," and that allows you to see the human side of things. Now, as a dad myself, it's my job to end that as best I can. And maybe my daughter, if she has kids, has to end a little bit of it, too, because something's going to trickle through. I'm not perfect and neither is my wife, and we don't claim to be. But it does put a level of humanity on those people that we're very angry with throughout our lives.

MC: You mentioned that he often put the onus on you for the responsibility of a failed relationship, which is simply nothing more than him projecting his own inadequacies onto someone else so that he doesn't have to accept them in himself. But it does make me go back and wonder if he suffered the same sort of idea about God that you and I did. I'm willing to bet that he probably suffered from the idea that God was absent in the same way his father was. So, there's all this psychological background that goes on, so much so that it's so easy to hold a grudge against someone until you sit down objectively and ask, "Where did they come from? What were their traumas?" And, you're right, it doesn't lessen their responsibility but it at least gives you some framework of understanding why they are the way they are. But, you're also right that each generation has a responsibility to be better, to do better, to give better to their children. And look, I know you and your family pretty well; I think your daughter has got a really good chance.

MJD: Well, thank you. We are trying to stack the deck in her favor.

MC: As you should. You know, it reminds me of something Peter Rollins once said, and I'll paraphrase: If you try to describe God, you immediately diminish him.[1] So, each and every one of us, in trying to understand God, is operating from a very specific point of view that only sees part of God. It does become difficult, then, to channel that, and to make it as much of a positive for your child as you can. And, of course that's true for every parent, even ours. Because, you know, I've had to forgive a lot of crap as well, or at least try to understand it. So, it does become a daunting process, unless you get out of your own way and allow that to happen. Unfortunately, it still has a very long-lasting effect on us. Even if we've come to a place of understanding, there's still the ramifications of emotional trauma along the way. And then, add into all this our ideas about religion, the ideas of hell and other concepts, and it becomes even more damaging. I was terrified of hell. I know I've heard you say that so many times. I don't think I ever had nightmares, but I know that you have mentioned having bad dreams or waking up frightened and thinking of hell.

MJD: Yeah, I had multiple recurring dreams. I had one where my grandfather was in something akin to the battle of Armageddon, and I was always there with him. I don't know if he died in every battle, but I remember carrying his body across the killing fields on numerous occasions. There was another—and I think my mom is convinced to this day that I was demon-possessed, and I would say to some degree, sure; it just depends on our ontology of demons—where I woke up and was running through the house yelling "Snake eyes!" There were all these serpents and demonic-type creatures, and my mom and stepdad got me down onto a chair while I was screaming at them. I didn't recognize anything at all, but I do vaguely remember that event, and I think it was due to my belief and my terror over what potentially awaited me, my family, and obviously my grandfather, who was a chief character in these dreams. So, needless to say, it was terrifying, and there were multiple instances throughout my childhood where I had those kinds of dreams. Now, I don't believe in that bullshit any longer and, lo and behold, those dreams have gone away.

MC: I've had that same experience, but of course people always want to tell me, "Well, you're no longer a threat to the devil, so he doesn't have to bother you."

MJD: Then, fine! So be it.

MC: Exactly. I guess he's the author of peace if he's now going to leave me alone. Just an observation, though; do you think that there's any validity to the idea that you had these hellish dreams your grandfather was always a part of because he wasn't a Christian? In other words, do you think he was a huge part of these dreams because of some subconscious fear?

MJD: Yes! Absolutely. I was terrified that he was going to go to hell. I was terrified to some degree for myself. However, I really tried to love Jesus, I tried to read my Bible and do all the noble things good Christian boys and girls do, but I knew he was very agnostic and apathetic toward the whole situation. I think like all Portuguese and other Mediterranean folks, he was raised Catholic, but that didn't mean anything, and I knew that because he never attended church and didn't talk about God. And in the Evangelical world, that's a backslidden or reprobate Christian, right? So, to that end, I was extremely terrified and thoroughly convinced that he was going to end up in hell. And so, I do believe that's why he specifically was the lead character in the tragedy known as my dreams.

MC: And it's ironic that you were with him. To my mind, it says a lot about where you thought you stood as well.

MJD: I'm glad you bring that up because I did feel as if I had this burden to proselytize. I had this burden to convert him before he passed away. I felt that. Being an introvert and being a child and not wanting to talk about these things because I was kind of embarrassed about them—all that combined for an extremely stressful situation.

MC: I don't mean to jump ahead in the timeline, but just out of curiosity, you said that your grandfather just died recently; did you ever have that conversation with him, or did you have conversations about that as you got older and wiser?

MJD: No, I didn't. And I don't live with any regret about that. We had a very loving relationship. He was a very loving man. He was loved by a lot of people. And, by the time I got into my mid to late twenties or so, I did not believe that that was something we had to do.

MC: Did he ever express any interest in God?

MJD: He was generally a pretty quiet man, and he didn't say too much about that. He did believe that he was going to see his deceased wife—she died about ten years before him—after he died. He did believe that. He believed in some sort of mystical experience. I don't think he believed in the "traditionally Christian" ideas of heaven and hell but believed there was some sort of afterlife.

MC: Fascinating. So, you had quite a bit in your early years, as far as the heaviness that often is associated with Christian beliefs. And that is a lot for a kid to handle or to carry around.

MJD: Yeah, we skipped the fluffy stages—the woo-woo Jesus-stuff.

MC: Was that present at all? Was that a part of your experience?

MJD: The charismatic stuff? No, none of that. And I think that's why I'm kind of repulsed by the whole charismatic movement. I never felt Jesus "in this place tonight." I never had that. Even as a musician, I liked a handful of the melodies and would "feel" the music sometimes—although the music was typically pretty bad—but I never felt the need to raise my hands or anything like that. I would never dance around. I would never have tears. Any emotion felt whatsoever was due to the melodic structure of the songs, but even that was minimal.

MC: Oh my God, I did all of that. All of it. That's a whole different side of the equation, but it still has its own expectations. And you know this because you're very much a student of mimetic theory—the idea of being in a large room of people that are doing things like that, there's an overwhelming urge to feel a part of the group. And so, you enter into it, especially when it's considered spiritual and good and Godly and all those things. Of course, you're going to enter into those kinds of things. But there's always that let-down afterwards.

MJD: And believe me, I felt the pull to do that precisely because of our mimetic nature. I could just never bring myself to do it, because, and you know me, I've never been a bullshitter. I'm not going to fake something. You pretty much know how Matt feels about everything. But I still felt almost obligated to do that because it's what everyone's feeling. Obviously, I would be missing something by not.

MC: Also, especially as a young kid or even one in their early teenage years, there's an expectation of you growing into those things; and yet, you're also having this experience with peer-pressure and wanting to fit in with your friends who don't have that experience. So, there's this sense of embarrassment, too. "God's expecting it, but I can't do it because of X, Y, and Z." In essence, you end up living in this dichotomous little world—of school-Matt and church-Matt—because you're trying to fit into a mold that's been specified for you. Often, that gets a little confusing and kind of splits your personality for a time. This is especially true in your early teenage years.

MJD: That is absolutely true.

MC: Okay, so you've put forth a lot in this session. I think people will have a good idea about where you come from. Shall we move onto your teenage years in the next session?

MJD: Yeah, because we've gotta talk about all the awkwardness that comes your way as you enter into those most formative years. We've gotta talk about porn and masturbation and girls and acne and all that fun stuff the church has little understanding of.

---

1. In *How (Not) to Speak of God*, Rollins introduces the idea that we must "embrace the a/theological approach that acknowledges the extent to which our supposed God-talk fails to define who or what God is" (Rollins, *How (Not) to Speak of God*, Introduction).

SEX, PURITY, AND CLUMSINESS

Session Three

Michelle Collins: Last time, we covered your early childhood and the emotional and psychological struggles that came with it, so this time we are going to move into your teenage years.

Matthew J. Distefano: Yes, let's get awkward!

MC: Well, the teenage years are rough regardless of circumstances, and then to throw in a bunch of religious fuckery on top of it . . .

MJD: You're right. Just biologically and physiologically-speaking, these years are kind of a clusterfuck. Hormones start kicking in at different times for different kids. I, for one, was a late bloomer. During my freshman year, I was probably 5′5″ and now I'm 6′4". So, my legs were constantly sore from all the growth pains, I had shin splints from time to time, and even have stretch marks from growing so fast. But, of course, on top of all that, if you have the religious baggage, if you have the shame, especially once you get into sexual issues—looking at porn, looking at girls (or guys, depending on what you're into)—it becomes a double-edged sword. It's already awkward, but then things become really bad because you're supposed to table this natural thing that happens—sexuality—until you're married, until Jesus approves of it. And I know it's probably worse for women, but, as a boy, it's in your face all the time. You still have to deal with the shame. You're still bombarded by guilt. You're not quite as "damaged goods" when you mess up, but it's still an issue.

MC: Correct. That tends to be more of a female perspective than a male one. But it's still damaging.

MJD: It's still damaging. The good thing is that the onus is on you women to protect us men by not dressing so scandalously, because we're obviously too weak. Honestly, y'all are just a problem.

MC: Well, I know you say that jokingly, but it brings up an interesting point. I've heard you say this before, and my former husband has even said it: *that* view is incredibly demeaning to men because it assumes men are incapable of controlling any of their baser urges. It assumes that they need to be coddled and protected, which kind of goes against the whole idea of patriarchy, if you ask me. I mean, I as a woman am supposed to protect *you* from this horrible thing and yet, you're supposed to be "the man." It's a very conflicting message, and I think as a kid that must force you to think, "What the hell am I supposed to do here?"

MJD: Yeah, it's kind of all over the map. You're right, on the one hand, we're the men so we have the power; we're in charge, but then we're not even capable of *not* touching women. Funny, that. On the other hand, though, we *should* be able to explore our urges in a healthy way.

In other words, if you look at certain images or think certain thoughts or even perform certain actions—with 1,000% consent, of course—it shouldn't become a shame festival the minute you do these things. So, we need to embrace that we are powerless in this fight, realize it's a natural thing, and then come up with healthy ways to explore our sexuality.

MC: It's a biological part of growing up.

MJD: Exactly. So, the question becomes, "How do we do this in a healthy way—healthy for boys, girls, men, women, and everyone in between?" Sadly, that's the key question that's missed by the Christian church at large. There's no healthy discussion about it; it's basically, "don't do this, don't do that, and force yourself to think about other things."

MC: It's a prohibitive thing.

MJD: Right. And it's essentially the premise for *Every Young Man's Battle*, which is a shit-show of a book that I had to read. It's basically this: don't touch yourself or look at anything that gives you a boner because it's bad and God's watching. That's the takeaway I had anyway.

MC: I know for me, the words "purity culture" were never uttered, but the ideas found in purity culture were definitely an expectation. Do you recall hearing that term, or how was that an expectation for you?

MJD: I never heard all of this categorized as "purity culture" until much later in life, but it very much was a culture of so-called purity. You had to be a virgin when you got married. You had to be a virgin on your wedding night. That was emphasized over and over. Our sermons were basically about the End Times or about not having sex. But what was funny is that there was always a work-around for the people around me. Kids were doing stuff: hand jobs under the covers, quick blowies after Bible studies, etc. There was way more sexual exploration than the pastors would have liked, even if it wasn't "intercourse." And, of course, we as humans—now that I've studied mimetic theory and understand basic psychology—find work arounds for just about everything. There are loopholes in everything. I remember this whole movement—and this is a legit thing that went on—of Mormons having anal sex because they would see that as not losing their virginity. Apparently, what matters is the vagina.

MC: Right. It's the sacred hymen. The goal is that that is an in-tact thing when you get married. That is the expression of purity for a female. There is no such thing as an expression of purity for a male. There's no obvious physical attribute that could clue anyone in. So, as a woman that's an expectation you have to take on. But this has been going on for a long time. I remember it being a prevalent thing when I was in high school. Anything that didn't involve actual vaginal intercourse was all good because you still could be considered "pure." Until, of course, we got to President Clinton and the whole Monica Lewinsky thing. That's when it got a little wonky because, c'mon, what are we really talking about here? In your teenage years, then, it's all about, "What can I get away with and still toe the line?"

MJD: Because in the church we're still working with a prohibition model. "Do not do this." *Okay, but how can I get right up next to it* *without crossing over.* Instead, we need to ask what a healthy sexuality looks like. But does the church even know? Do pastors even know? Of course not. It was a joke when my wife and I had premarital counseling. It was an absolute joke. There was no depth. If anything, we should have met with a licensed sex therapist, because the pastor we met with was obviously not trained in any real way other than some Christian counseling courses, which are not real courses at all.

MC: They had an ordination, that's all.

MJD: It's just so silly. When we have a prohibition model, we always tend toward pushing the envelope of what we can get away with and still call ourselves pure. And look, it's whatever; it's just not a healthy way to express yourself sexually and doesn't aid you in growing up one iota.

MC: So, personal question: Did you go into your marriage in the way you were supposed to?

MJD: You mean, was I a virgin? Yes.

MC: Really?

MJD: Really. I didn't even get a blow job or a hand job. All my friends were getting blowies or hand jobs under the covers, but not me.

MC: Wow! I'm impressed.

MJD: You should be! That was the one thing I didn't do. I did drugs and stuff, but never had sex.

MC: So, that brings up an interesting topic, as far as this stuff goes. Because we're talking about the pre-teen and teenage years—and it's not just about sex, though that's a big topic—we have to talk about drugs and other vices because that's a very big no-no as well. Did you have that in your life? Was that another lecture or sermon that was presented to you that you had to struggle with?

MJD: I don't remember any "don't do drugs" sermons during those years. It was kind of assumed that we wouldn't do that because it was illegal anyway. You weren't really going to have to do a sermon on not doing cocaine because it just seemed obvious, even though it really wasn't. But there is this pick and choose methodology in the church when it comes to which sins are to be emphasized. We all hear the phrase, "all sins are weighted equally," but that's not *really* the case, right? We're not talking about the sin of violence, or even something like gossip or eating yourself to death. We're basically only concerned with sex and not being gay because that's all we tend toward emphasizing. I mean, I had pastors who would brag about how many Vicodin they had to take after a surgery, while condemning anyone who smoked weed. And for me, it was just so silly. They picked and chose what they wanted to pick and choose, and sex was just one of the main ones, if not *the* main one. But not only sex—any sort of lust. Right?

MC: The problem here is that because any semblance of sexuality was so demonized, or just so emphasized in the negative, it has created quite a lot of people with very negative viewpoints about sex, even as they get married. What the purity culture says is that you're supposed to be pure until you get married, and then all of a sudden, the proverbial lightbulb will turn. This has no basis in reality, though. I have spent time talking with people that *did* wait until they were married and on their honeymoon were horribly disappointed. There was physical and emotional pain, there were hurt feelings, and they ended up in some kind of therapy for it because their expectations didn't happen. Why? All that tension was still there because sex had always been a negative in their minds. We actually create neural pathways for that stuff. It's brain science. And so, we've done a lot of damage in the name of purity. Unfortunately, you're talking about a time in life when already your brain is taking in so much and your growth is so much in flux, and now you're creating these new neural pathways about negative situations with sex, and those are hard to break as you get older. To that end, there is a lot of guilt and shame that goes along with the whole subject. The one thing that always struck me, or strikes me now anyway, is that in the Bible we're told that the strength of sin is the Law, because as soon as we say something is wrong, we have created an object of desire, and you know that with mimetic theory. We've created an object of desire and now we're constantly at odds with ourselves to try and control our baser instincts. So, as a kid, that's a lot of pressure. It's damaging.

MJD: It's a lot of pressure and it does a lot of damage and has its tendrils in your life decades later, so much so that you don't even recognize it until much later. That has been true for my wife and I. It's just during these last three or four years that we've really been able to be more sexually open and free, and I think a lot of that has to do with our upbringing and the view that was placed on us about sex and what sex is supposed to look like or how sex is supposed to feel. To think that you can turn it on like a light switch the night you get married or even a month later!? No. You have created trauma—true trauma—that you cannot undo as if you're untying your shoelaces.

MC: I think that's a very good point because often we forget how anything that creates shame in us is automatically trauma-inducing. Shame and trauma go hand in hand. And so, there are trauma responses, which is why you'll have those triggered moments. As I've shared with you before, my background involves sexual abuse, so when it came to sex in marriage, there were triggered reactions that happened. And I didn't have the bandwidth to describe or explain this. That causes a lot of problems. It was not until perhaps three or four years ago that I finally threw that off and said, "I don't give a shit anymore." And think about this: as a teenager, you're starting to learn about sexuality, you're also living in a church environment where you're told that God is always watching you. Well, that will screw your head up just a little bit! I don't need God watching me do anything.

MJD: Yeah, that is a really, really creepy image that we paint in our minds or in the minds of others. It's really unfortunate, and it's one of those things you have to deconstruct that you don't initially think you'll have to deconstruct. It's one of those "other beliefs" that comes about that you didn't realize would relate. And then, it's as if you can't help but see how everything is related. Ultimately, though, this is a good thing.

MC: Absolutely. There's some freedom in that—when you start to realize how much is interconnected. Here, you thought you'd just wrestle with some of the things you believed about Christianity or about God, and then suddenly you've gone across this entire spectrum to where you're deconstructing yourself, everything from your sex life to your relationships to how you view yourself—everything. Everything comes into focus and you realize how interrelated this has all been. I don't remember if I've said this to you or not, but as Christians you're taught that who you are in Christ is your identity, so when you begin to shed those viewpoints, your identity comes into question and your sexual identity is one of those things. Interestingly, then, most people, even as adults, don't feel comfortable talking honestly about this subject. It's considered taboo or private, but maybe we should talk about it more because I think there's a lot of people who would feel a lot freer and perhaps even realize they're not as broken as they thought they were.

MJD: It's one of those things where we need to find balance. There are certain things that should be private. At the same time, however, you're right; for some reason, in this culture—call it Western Christianity—sex is still taboo. And we need to open up more. We need to start talking about it in healthier ways. And we start by stripping away the shame. We have to take shame out of the equation and acknowledge that true vulnerability looks like this: being able to share your deepest desires or darkest secrets with someone without being made to feel as if what you desire is shameful. Really, there should be nothing wrong with so-called weirdness, with so-called kink, or with anything like that.

MC: Like you said, some things are private, but certainly between people who now are in a relationship, that subject should be allowed to be open. Conversations without judgement should be front and center. Of course, that means both people need to be in a healthy place as it pertains to sexuality. If one person is still very much religious in their mindset, while the other person is deconstructing or has deconstructed, you can end up with some relationship issues. Those, you'll have to work through, but gently.

MJD: Moving forward, then, we have to start by changing how we talk about this in our teenage years. We have to start teaching healthier sexuality from the get-go, which will only stack the deck in people's favor.

MC: Right. Switching gears, now; other than sex, what else stands out for you during these most formidable years? What else impacted you?

MJD: I was never one to be satisfied by shallow answers, so my teenage years built upon the early questions I had about God and the relationship I had with God. That is to say, I was never in a place where I was comfortable. I was never comfortable with the ideas about God that I held. This caused me to become more aggravated during my teenage years because you start to explore who you are as a person, you start to explore who you are in relation to other people, and you start to push back against God because your experiences aren't lining up with the things you've been told about . . . well, anything. Early on in life, you might have cute, little questions that niggle at you but tend to go away pretty quickly. But your teenage years, and I've heard Richard Rohr talk about this, are more like the prophetic tradition found in the Bible. You're more in the book of Lamentations, always shaking your fist at the sky. Early childhood is more like the Law—don't do this, don't do that, don't touch the stove or you're going to get burned—but the teenage years are more like the Prophets. And sure, you're not always left with the greatest of answers, but you're certainly pushing back against the things you find intolerable. My teenage years were a lot of that—a lot of, "this doesn't seem right." For one example, I had friends who killed themselves in high school, which meant I was now confronted with death and hell in a very real way. It's not just theoretical any longer. It's not just pining about where I'm going, or where my grandfather *might* go. Now it's real, and it's one of my friends who might be there. And let's be real: suicide was *one*, if not *the* unpardonable sin in the church. These sorts of things really cause you to not be able to put any questions to the side. They become something that resides in the forefront of your mind.

MC: Do you think that those kinds of experiences served as a way to double-down on your fears about hell? I would think they would have to. Because now you're reevaluating what happened with a friend and how that applies to you.

MJD: Yeah. It becomes really real. Any time someone dies, you're forced to consider your own mortality as well. And I don't care how old or how comfortable in life you are, when someone close to you dies, you start to think about those sorts of things a little more. To that end, when you're already in a place where you're thinking that hell is a possibility, it only exacerbates your anxieties.

MC: And as a kid, that's pretty harsh. First of all, as a child, or even a teenager, having thoughts of hell and the terror that invokes, is rough. But then having that compounded by a suicide—that's even worse because you are then forced to reevaluate your own standing with God. I know people react differently. Some have that Christian task list, so to speak; they have to get serious about things so that they show themselves approved. But others do the opposite. Did you have any coping mechanisms that you had as a teenage that helped you deal with your relationship with God, especially in the face of something like that?

MJD: I tried. I really tried. The Bible was emphasized quite highly, and so I tried to do Bible studies. I tried to engage. I tried to have a more robust prayer life. Busy work, you know? I just couldn't do it, because I knew I was being fake. And look, I know there is that old adage, "fake it until you make it," but I just couldn't fake it for very long. So, obviously I never "made it." My later teenage years and then into my early twenties, I played worship music. And I liked music, so I could fake that better than prayer or Bible studies. I didn't like Christian music by any stretch of the imagination, but I liked playing. I liked playing multiple instruments. That was, to me, a way to be right with God because I could at least say that I led some people to him. Even if I wasn't having the experience at the time, I facilitated it for others.

MC: So, perhaps you'd get a pass . . .

MJD: Exactly. If I was going to hell, maybe it wouldn't be as torment-ing. Music was my way of contributing something when I couldn't seem to have any sort of emotional attachment to God. Honestly, I don't know if I earnestly worshipped more than five times while play-ing "worship" music. I just didn't feel much. But, again, I facilitated, so that was the task I could check off the list.

MC: You've noted that you tried to feel God but couldn't. While people raised their hands and did all the things that we've come to expect in an Evangelical worship service, you couldn't. That's kind of unusual, especially as you consider the idea of mimetic theory and teenage peer pressure on top of it. To be in that environment, and to be not able to function in that way . . . it's interesting. Why do you think that was not something you were able to do?

MJD: I don't know if it's just our different physiological processes, or what. I don't know if some of us are just better at faking it. I'm not saying everyone fakes it, but I know it goes on.

MC: Everyone fakes it.

MJD: Okay, I stand corrected. However, I can't say that it's all fake because I'm certain people have experiences where they feel emotional and overwhelmed, and I've seen people crying in services. I don't know, though. I'm not sure why some people feel it, others fake it, and yet others like myself say "fuck it." I can talk about it from a mimetic theory standpoint and say much of what goes on is a mimetic thing. But, at the same time, for some of us, we still can't bring ourselves to desire that and are even somewhat repulsed by it. Even if I noticed my friends desiring God while allowing a worship service to impact them in a profound way, I never felt a damn thing. Maybe it's something in our "wiring." Some of us simply aren't good bullshitters. I've never been a good bullshitter.

MC: I was a very good bullshitter. I was very involved in all that. I had no problems doing any of that. And like you said, some of it comes back to mimetic theory, but I had those experiences on my own as well. Now, looking back, however, I am forced to ask, how much of that was actual body chemicals and processes, as well as brain science? When there's an expectation of an outcome, we tend to manifest that outcome. I'm not going to say it's bad. I think people enjoy it. I don't know if it's any different than a drug.

MJD: And it doesn't mean it's not real. When I tell people that when it comes to the Charismatics, a lot of it can be explained by mimetic theory, I don't mean it's not real. It's very real. I'm just explaining *why* it happens—typically when you're at church, typically when there's a bunch of other people. It doesn't take away the validity of how real it is for people. For some of us, though, we get disenfranchised and disillusioned when it's not real for us. Then we have to ask the questions: "What's wrong with *me*? What am *I* doing wrong? Why can't *I* feel this?" It reminds me of a girlfriend I had in my late teenage years, whose mantra was basically, "Jesus! Jesus! Jesus! Jesus!" She shed tears at every worship service—was kind of spastic and jolty. And I remember asking: "Is there something wrong with me? Is this what I'm supposed to be doing?" Worse, though, was when I would then compare myself to Jesus and realize I was doing nothing for her compared to him.

MC: If only you could measure up to Jesus.

MJD: If only. But I was failing with God and I was failing with her.

MC: And we're talking about a time when you're so self-conscious anyway. You're so consumed with the idea that everyone is looking at you and you're failing to measure up. So, now you had this added element of trying to please God, who is apparently always watching, while feeling nothing for him. So, yes, the automatic assumption is, "I'm broken. Something *is* wrong with me." In the church, however, we can't tell anyone that. We have to be "okay." And so, some people fake it 'til they make it.

MJD: It all comes back to shame. If you aren't "okay," you're going to be shamed.

MC: Exactly. You're not a part of the group. You're an outsider. You're a weirdo and an outcast. Especially in that time of your life, when you haven't reached the mental maturity yet to be okay with yourself. And I don't even know when that is, and I'm sure it's different for every person, but it's certainly not in your teenage years. Your brain is not even fully developed yet. And, of course, that's stuff we learn as we get older, but we don't know that then. We felt like we were fully functioning humans when we were teenagers. You don't find out until later that you're only partly a person, for a lack of a better way to put it. So, the teenage years are pretty difficult anyways, but with the added pressure of a religious, Christian context, it gets even harder. It's not surprising that it's a difficult time.

MJD: Not to mention that the so-called "age of accountability" is so young. You're not even allowed to be a screw-up as a teenager, because you're now accountable in the same way some thirty, forty, or fifty-year-old adult is accountable. That's quite a burden to place on a child or adolescent.

MC: It's a lot of responsibility at an age when you're probably not very responsible.

MJD: To think that some twelve or thirteen-year-old is responsible for their eternality—where their ultimate, eternal destination is going to be—is mind-blowingly stupid.

MC: In hindsight, of course it's ludicrous. Looking back, though, I remember when my children were getting older and just having that false sense of security that they weren't at "that" age yet, so if they died, they would be okay. When I think back on that now, first of all I'm embarrassed. But second of all, I'm horrified that that was my mindset. Even as a parent, when you have a teenager, you're dealing with a whole different level of emotion when there's a religious influence involved. It's not just if your kid is going to get in trouble, it's, "Are they going to go to hell? And am I responsible for that as their parent?" So, there's so much that goes into this discussion. We typically only look at it from the perspective of being a teenager, but not those raising them.

MJD: I haven't quite gotten there yet, but I at least know I'm not going to have to worry about some stupid age of accountability.

MC: And again, you're doing your daughter a great service. So, this seems like a good place to stop for now. We can transition from the awkward teenage years to the less awkward, albeit still uncomfortable, early adult ones. We're going to get a little more into the philosophical mindset of an early adult.

MJD: That sounds perfect.

THE FALLING OF THE HOUSE OF CARDS

Session Four

Michelle Collins: So, we've covered the early stuff. We've covered your interesting teenage years, and all the sex-talk.

Matthew J. Distefano: They weren't any more interesting than anyone else's.

MC: These years play an important role, though. Obviously. Generally speaking, the teenage years play an important part because a lot of thought formulation happens at that time. However, it's interesting to note how your brain is not fully developed. So, you have teenagers who think they know it all, only to find out later that they didn't know a damn thing. The astounding part is this: at that age, when you do think you know everything, you're also developing your sexuality. So, you have all these compounding issues that then become a little more in-depth the older you get. Then you look back and realize that you really *were* clueless. On top of that, if you throw religion in there, things just get even more dicey.

MJD: You're absolutely right. Even in your early twenties, it is kind of a perfect-storm situation where—and I don't know if this is the case for women—you're not thinking with your undeveloped mind, but with your genitals much of the time. In other words, you have these urges, you have these sexual desires that come into play, and then, you don't even know what's going on at all in spite of the fact that you think you do. Maybe you have a little confidence, maybe you start having to shave your pathetic, sorry excuse for a moustache or something, and you're feeling pretty good with your new sense of freedom, but you really don't know what the hell is going on.

MC: It's a confusing time, for sure. Even if we think back about other subjects—maybe people who are thinking that their sexuality is a little bit "different" than what the prescribed norm is—then we should realize it's an even tougher time for them. They're coming into this age where they're trying to figure all that out anyway, and then they're thrown a curveball, so to speak. And it's not okay to talk about, or so we're told. Interestingly enough, I came across a conversation the other day where a kid who knew he was gay as he was growing up, who lived in a family who was very accepting of that—he wasn't religious at all, there was no problems that way—and yet he still struggled to actually admit that about himself. So, that's how deeply engrained the sexual "status quo" is. I thought that was interesting. Throwing all this kind of stuff into the teenage years, you come to some understanding of who you think you are, and now you're stepping into early adulthood with this understanding behind you. And now you have even more responsibility, as far as work, as far as family, as far as religion. We haven't talked too much about the age of accountability, but you're definitely there by the time you're an adult.

MJD: Yeah, typically I think the age of accountability is younger for most denominations. Some put it at twelve, some older like fifteen or sixteen, and some even younger like eight, nine, or ten. Regardless, there is this sense of double responsibility after that point. You're now a young adult. You're in the church so perhaps you're mentoring some teenagers because you just went through it and have become a de facto expert, which is fairly ludicrous. For me, this was the formula: graduate high school, go to college and get a bachelor's degree, and then get married right away so you can finally use your penis in a more appropriate manner—you know, without the guilt and shame. I think this is pretty typical among Evangelicals. You get married pretty young and start having a bunch of babies. That's how it was in my church; I'm not sure what it was like for you.

MC: I did get married young. My experience wasn't necessarily church-related, but I had my first child at twenty-two.

MJD: I don't know if it's always church-related, but for my church this formula was fairly common. This was especially true for girls. You had to be a young mom and go to young mom groups and all those things.

MC: There is also the idea that is left over from times past. You go back quite a ways and you see girls were married pretty young. Several hundred years ago, they were married at thirteen or fourteen. So, there's some holdover mentality associated with that. Essentially, *this is your lot in life*. This is especially true if you're coming from a religious background. Your whole identity is rolled up into the idea of being a "Proverbs 31 woman." This is preached at you constantly—sexual

41

purity and all those things. So, if you want to be sexually pure, it makes sense to get married younger because you don't have to hold out as long. And it's your job! It's literally your job to get married, have children, and take care of a household so that your husband doesn't have to worry about those things. So, those are some leftover mentalities that are still prevalent in a lot of congregations, especially the more conservative-minded.

MJD: And if you have this unhealthy view of sexuality and then get married young, as we said in the last session, you're not going to be able to switch things on like a light switch. For me, that played into this whole process. Not only did I have the continued questions—theologically and philosophically—moving from my teenage years to my early twenties, but I then had the problems that occur when two people who marry young have unhealthy views of sexuality. You have a type of struggle that doesn't get resolved until you get real with shit. And that takes time. Sometimes, it takes a long time!

MC: A long while in most cases, I would say. It wasn't until I was older when I said, "Hold on! Some stuff needs to be dealt with." And, of course, I also had a lot of other mitigating circumstances, but I think that, coming from a woman's perspective, you are almost trained that this is your lot in life: As long as your husband doesn't assault you in some way, you have it good and you should just not complain. And then you have to look at the responsibility level on the men's side: Now you have a family, now you have to get your shit together, now you have to take care of people, etc. You have to suddenly be "a man," when maybe you don't have all the tools yet. Maybe you don't have the bandwidth to actually fill that role, much of which comes from your father. But, to complicate matters, when your father is not there, how does one learn to become this "man of God" that they're supposed to be? Well, they're pretty much having to do so by the dictates of the church. It becomes a very one-sided perspective.

MJD: You make an interesting point that the woman's lot in life is to just be there for the husband. And that's true in the church, broadly speaking. I honestly don't understand how any man can desire that for their partner. It makes no sense. You should be miserable if your spouse is not content, not happy, not "doing their thing." If I knew my partner was sexually unhappy, unhappy with their job, with whatever, I don't know how you can default to, "well, it's your role as a woman." And we heard this growing up: it's the wife's role to satisfy her husband sexually. Well, what about *her* sexual satisfaction? This rote sexual role should offend us. It did for me. If I just want to think selfishly: How would it feel, knowing that my partner isn't sexually satisfied? This should really piss us off.

MC: It should. But remember, oftentimes the environment in your religious background is associated with the ideas of patriarchy. It's your right to be in control. Your woman just needs to get over it and do her job. These are longstanding thoughts, so, in my estimation, the fact that you can't see it that way is commendable. Unfortunately, there's far too many men who think it's perfectly acceptable.

MJD: I just can't relate to that. It sounds repulsive to me.

MC: I would agree. I had a conversation not too long ago with someone who had a disagreement with her husband over something personal—she was changing clothes or something—and he took a picture of her without her permission; and when she said, "that's objectionable," his response was, "but it's my right." That's a prevalent mindset. Obviously, I would disagree and there would be a throwdown if it had been me.

MJD: As there should've been.

MC: He would have had my fingers around his neck. But regardless, it speaks to the mindset. It speaks to that specifically being a part of the conversation in conservative, religious households. So, as you move into young adulthood or the marriage relationship, you're bringing along all these preconceived ideas and notions of this conservative, religious idealism that's going to have a drastic effect on your marriage in one way or another. Either it's going to become an abusive situation that ends in divorce, or it's going to become a scenario where the man goes along, thinking everything's fine while the woman's miserable for the entire marriage.

MJD: Or, things come to a head, and you both start to deconstruct. This is one of the things that we've touched on. This is one of the areas that get deconstructed that you don't initially think needs to. You might know that there are some things to work on, but it's actually one of those things that often needs to be torn down and built back up again entirely. When it comes to deconstruction, we tend to think theologically: What do I think about this doctrine? What do I think about that creedal statement? What do I think about the Bible? But then in comes this sort of thing. In comes the deconstruction of marriage. And the problematic thing is that you kind of have to do it together because you're in it together.

MC: Of course. And you know this: the deconstruction process is not always equal on a linear timeline.

MJD: It typically isn't.

MC: Right. So, one will reach some place before the other, which of course then causes some issues. It was very difficult for me and my former husband, and still is sometimes, because you are questioning different things at a different time and from a different perspective. It can then become something that is very upsetting. But let's go back a little bit. How old were you when you got married?

MJD: Twenty-one.

MC: So, you were young.

MJD: I was very young. I was about to turn twenty-two. My wife is a couple months younger than I am. We were both twenty-one. I moved out of my house a few months before we got married, and I lived by myself in a shitty apartment before my wife moved in.

MC: She moved in before you got married?

MJD: No, no, no, Michelle! We were good Christians. We weren't going to live in sin!

MC: I'm going to make an assumption here, so correct me if I'm wrong, but your wife was of course raised in the church as well, right?

MJD: Very heavily so. Her grandfather was a pastor of a Christian and Missionary Alliance church for—God, I can only guess—twenty or thirty years.

MC: So, she obviously came into the relationship with a lot of her own religious baggage, or religious perspective.

MJD: And definitely raised more fundamentalist than I was.

MC: And yet, you've mentioned to me that you've always had this philosophical mind, which doesn't always bode well when pitted against any sort of fundamentalism. Can you unpack that a little more for me? What does that mean for you?

MJD: Well, I always loved my critical thinking courses in college. I've always loved logic (and not just the rapper). I've always loved studying philosophy in undergrad. So, I was always thinking about these existential questions and what my faith meant to me, and how it worked in real time—basically always unpacking what we say about life, God, the universe, and how all these ideas worked together. Of course, not everyone was doing this. So, I had all these questions that I kicked around in my head throughout my early twenties: If God is like *this*, what does that mean for us? If God is supposedly violent, why is our violence so repulsive when we see it play out in the real world? How can we say that people freely damn themselves to hell when I work in group homes and see that these kids are not "free?" You know, the questions that really look at our theological theories to see how they really play out.

MC: So, you were comfortable with questions?

MJD: I was very comfortable with questions, but I wasn't comfortable with the depth of answers I received.

MC: Were you outwardly vocal about your questions about God?

MJD: Not in my early twenties, but maybe in my mid to late twenties. I started to become a little more vocal or outgoing in terms of what I thought. But they were still pretty tame compared to where I'm at now.

MC: Well, you're a complete heretic now.

MJD: I prefer the term apostate these days. *Heretic!* came out in 2018; *Apostate!* is the forthcoming sequel.

MC: So, as it pertained to your relationship with your wife: Was your wife on board with that? Was she a questioner? Or was she more set with where she was at?

MJD: Her case is pretty interesting because like me, she was certainly never as fundamentalist as her church or parents or grandparents. She was involved but was always unsure about what she was being told—hell and things like that—but she was never vocal about it. And she was a little bit uncomfortable, not so much with me having the questions, but when I started vocalizing them. Because then it comes to a head with the family dynamic, and they start taking screenshots of what your husband says on Facebook and they start sharing it with pastors and other family members. Let me rephrase: they printed things out because they're not tech-savvy.

MC: So, that almost becomes a situation where there is a loyalty question. That is, "Am I loyal to my husband or loyal to my family and God?"

MJD: It was more between me and her family than me and God, because she was okay with my theological questioning. She's had the same sorts of questions throughout her life but just never vocalized them. Her family, though, took everything personally. They took my questioning as a personal attack, but it was never that. I guess I can see how it could be taken that way, though. When you abandon your faith, when you abandon your church, people get worried about your soul and I guess there is something commendable in that.

MC: I always find that to be a bit inauthentic, simply because if that were the case, they would be a lot more demonstrative in their attempts to pull people away from the gates of hell. I think what's really happening in situations like these is a dose of cognitive dissonance. They're trying to return to a normal state of mind, and your questioning threatens them. It threatens them on a very deep level so they have to dismiss it or explain it way. Either that or they have to get really personal with their questions and that's terribly uncomfortable, as we both know. It's interesting to me the various responses we get from different relationships, simply based on question asking. It's wildly ironic that you're supposed to be loved and accepted by your family, first and foremost, and yet they're often the ones who attack first in situations like this.

MJD: I think you're correct about it being inauthentic because who better to seek out than the one who backslid and fell away from the church? So, if you *really* cared about these eschatological scenarios or where others are going when they die, then they would be going after the people who walked away from church and were the biggest questioners, because what a great testimony that would be!

MC: But it's usually that you're ostracized or excommunicated or whatever word you want to use. So, you end up in this place in the very early part of your life and you're still not even fully an adult.

MJD: Right. It's around twenty-five where our brains are fully developed. And so, you start asking these questions around that age and you're already having to unpack a lot of shit before you even get going.

MC: Exactly. And these are questions that you thought perhaps you already answered or already settled on at an earlier time, so it's kind of daunting. The emotion behind it is very upsetting because it is a mental game. It's like getting taken out at the knees mentally, and suddenly you're having to ask all these very difficult questions. And so, you had mentioned some of these questions that you had in your early adulthood—why is God allowed to be so violent?—but I never thought about that when I was younger. I just accepted that that was the way God is. But, then again, I had a very violent background so to me that was pretty normal. But I think that is a brilliant question and it's worthy of an answer. Of course, now, looking back in hindsight, I look at it and say, "if that's the kind of God he is, he is not worthy of worship."

MJD: And literally, sometimes you can't worship. You can fake it, but you know you're faking it. I remember asking a question at a Bible study during my twenties: "Are we sure God is okay with slavery?" Because, in the Bible, it's there. And people have used it to justify slavery as late as, well, the present day. I wouldn't say rightfully so, but you can make the case that it *is* biblical. Crazily, you can make that case. I obviously wasn't comfortable with that sort of thing, so I asked if we are sure this is what God wanted at that time, and the response was something like, "well, you see, the Hebrew people back then treated their slaves better," blah, blah, blah. This was one of those unsatisfactory answers I got when I was younger. And I'm not even a Black person. I couldn't imagine hearing such bullshit as a Black person.

MC: It also raises the question: "If it's biblical, and defensible with the Bible, are we then going against the Bible when we end slavery?"

MJD: Ouch.

MC: But again, you question these things and what you're really doing is getting into the ideas about infallibility. Are the "holy Scriptures" what we're supposed to live our lives by? But that's a question I got into much later, and not in my early adulthood. Like I said, I never even confronted the issue of God being violent; I was just terrified that he was. But I had been conditioned that way.

MJD: I wasn't necessarily as conditioned in that way. My mom and stepdad certainly didn't do that. They probably had some of the same questions, I'm guessing. I don't know, though; they just seemed to go with the rote lines.

MC: Well, what are you going to do?

MJD: I don't know. I don't know if some of us are just wired differently to be questioning and vocal like that. Myers-Briggs. Enneagram. All that stuff.

MC: I think that's true. I think there are people where that is the way they work and think. And I do think that eventually that comes out, even if you've been conditioned through religion for that to not happen; because there's an internal dialogue that's happening long before the external dialogue begins. My former husband has said the same thing. What happens is that these questions are forming and there's a case being built psychologically, and then one day you have to say something. It's an evolution.

MJD: That's been my experience, too. These questions were internal, and they would go around and around and around for years, decades even. They started out in simplistic forms, just little blips on the radar. But then, it's like how a snowball turns into an avalanche. Eventually, everything comes to a point where you step back and think, "I've just got to say this shit. I just have to be brave." I mean, for real, if you think about it, how can you *not* say something? You're telling me that God really said to kill all the children and animals when folks were warring? Or, that in Genesis, he flooded babies who didn't make it on the ark? Were we really not all wrestling with this shit? I guess some people weren't, but I can't help to think they were and were just really lying about it. Or, maybe they were just stuck in a place where these questions were still just little blips on their radar. I don't know. I'll tell you, though: I was pretty shocked by the dismissiveness when I first started vocalizing my questioning. I expected to be disagreed with to some degree, but I didn't expect the dismissiveness to be so off handed. I mean, God was turning people into pillars of salt because they disobeyed. I had disobeyed thousands of times and was never turned into salt. God really wanted a dude to go up on a mountain to murder his son? I would never think to test someone like that. So, my point being, there were all these stories that I couldn't wrap my mind around, and the church folks around me didn't seem to mind them at all. It was kind of fucked-up, to be honest, and I had nothing to relate them to. My dad wouldn't have even done those things. He did some shitty things, but nothing like that. That's some next-level shit.

MC: I don't know if this is true for you, but I've put myself in some of those types of situations and thought, "What if God asks me to do that? What would I do?" Well, I'd fail miserably. Then I was tortured with the idea that God would disown me, or that I would go to hell. So, there's all of these thought processes that take place when you even consider those questions, because if you honestly believed that God was this way, you'd have to consider those questions. The thought pattern goes like this: If Abraham was challenged in this way, I could be challenged in this way. That leads to some pretty ugly ideas.

MJD: And constant existential crises.

MC: And, of course, we could look at it from a different viewpoint and think that God would've known that he would stop short, but Abraham didn't know at the time. If we're going strictly by what God said to Abraham and what Abraham understood, he would have thought that he has to kill his child. And so, we can't even justify it that way, that it wasn't really God's intent because Abraham didn't know that. It all becomes very dark. To me, it becomes a very ethical thing to question those ideas. It is ethical and moral to say, "Hold on, God, why do you get to be an asshole while I'm held to a different standard?"

MJD: I think Matthew Korpman[1] would agree with you.

MC: Yes, he would. But seriously, why do I have to forgive my enemies and pray for those who curse me while he gets to burn his in hell forever? Of course, there's always the apologists that will say that God doesn't choose that; they choose it. But you can't get past the idea that if you believe in that kind of thing—eternal conscious torment—God had to create it. Whether it was originally made for people or not, that's what it's evolved to. And so, you have to really wrestle with the ethics of God. And I think that during that time in your life is when you do start actually wrestling with some of that stuff, unless you're just completely indoctrinated. And I'll admit, I was pretty much completely indoctrinated. It didn't occur to me that God could be a bad guy. I didn't understand any of it, but it's just the way it was. So, toe the line, or else. Did it change your behavior when you started having those questions?

MJD: I'm sure it did in some way. While I was having the initial questions, I don't think it changed my behavior or my level of loyalty to my friends. I was angry with the church because I felt betrayed. I felt that even with just a bit of studying or self-reflection, they wouldn't have been this dismissive and acted so arrogant about these things. I mean, they couldn't have told me that Left Behind theology came out in the 1800s? I knew they knew that. They always bragged about going to school. So, I was upset, because if they told me the truth, maybe I wouldn't have had these horrible nightmares growing up. But, as far as my behavior towards my family and friends, nothing really changed on my end. People did distance themselves from me because I was pretty vocal about my questions, so they made it clear to me that their behavior was going to change. I was still the same guy, though. I still wanted to hang out with them. I still wanted to be their friend. But having newly discovered, contradictory beliefs makes people uncomfortable. I guess you can't be the borderline atheist who used to be a Christian and still hang out with your Christian friends. I didn't determine that; they did.

MC: It reminds me of an example I use in my first book: *The Metamorphosis* by Kafka. In it, the main character was changing into a beetle, and no one could understand him. He spoke a different language. He looked differently. He lived differently. And they tried the plastic smiles for a while. His family tried. But eventually they begin to be angry with him. They begin to be dismissive to him, until finally he dies, and they just go on with their lives as if he never existed. And I think a lot of this process for me has felt like that. When I started questioning people in church, and my questions started becoming vocal, I got the very plastic responses. But then people started distancing themselves because they have to protect themselves. We're suddenly perceived as a threat to the tribe.

MJD: So, maybe it's better to start asking these questions earlier and get it all out of the way so you can move on with your life.

MC: And maybe move on with your life with the ability to ask more questions and be freer to do so, as opposed to living almost in a servant-mindset, which of course is heralded as something wonderful in Christendom.

MJD: Yeah, but you can take a "truth" and then twist it. And that's all that's happening there. We're to be servants under our own free volition, not under the threat of something or under coercion of some sort. Much of what the church has done is hammered home the servant ethic with the threat of the consigliere showing up at your door because the Don didn't get his payment.

MC: Which is ironic because Jesus calls us his friends, not his servants. My point being that there is in fact all these things that get changed and emphasized over other valid things that Jesus taught. But it didn't occur to me to ask the hard questions when I was younger. Honestly, I just sat with them and was okay with whatever was drilled into my head. So, I think it's commendable that in your early adulthood, you were actually able to say, "hold on, wait a minute, I have some questions."

MJD: And I don't know what it is, call it different callings, call it different biology, call it different genetics or upbringing, but some people just start earlier, and some don't start until their sixties or seventies. I've been talking to people lately who say that what I'm talking about in my books or online resonates with them because they've just started questioning things; and they could be my dad or even older. It's weird. I wonder what they're thinking, talking to what is for them a young kid (though I'm not *that* young any longer).

MC: But you've had these experiences that can help validate what they're experiencing. And we've talked about this already: there is no age requirement on this process. It's when each individual person is ready to take the trip.

MJD: Right. I've already mentioned how Richard Rohr clarifies this, but I'll reiterate: When he talks about the second half of life, it has nothing to do with age.

MC: No, nothing. It would be nice if there was a delineating time-frame, where you go from point A to point B to point C and so on.

MJD: The age thing is probably a bell curve of some sort, which means most fall somewhere in the middle, but not everyone.

MC: Probably. For myself, sometimes I lament how so much time was wasted. I lived in a trapped state of mind for so many years, and now I feel that being outside of that has its good and its bad. There's a whole world out there to explore but then there's those moments of, "what if I'm wrong?" It's almost like PTSD, a triggering fear that God is this vindictive, angry asshole that's going to send me to hell. So, had I done this when I was younger, maybe I would have had time to feel a little more at peace.

MJD: You're probably right, because I haven't had that thought in a long time.

MC: They don't come as often as they used to, but they still show up. It's not fun.

MJD: None of this is fun. None of this is easy. None of this can be scripted. It's different for everyone even if there are similarities in the overarching narrative. Obviously, the more people that have these conversations, the better. Just the fact that others can hear our stories and perhaps resonate with some of it—even if some is also different for them—is a benefit.

MC: Yeah, and that's why I hesitate with any kind of plan, or anything that says, "How to deconstruct," or any other derivation, because the thing that everyone shares is the emotion of it all, but not necessarily the exact experiences. We all come from a different mindset or belief system, and all have different personalities and familial situations. But, across the board, there is usually some similarity in the emotion that we're experiencing in the process itself, which has become fascinating to me. This is where we can find some common ground. So, even if I'm not deconstructing the same things that you are deconstructing, we can find some common ground in the fact that we're both experiencing some sort of emotion over the process itself, which is why it felt very much like it became a grieving process for me.

MJD: It's almost like you say in your first book, right? It resembles the grief cycle.

MC: It is. And it's funny because the more you say that to people, the more you point it out, they can't help but agree. And they may have different levels of experience with each of those periods of the cycle, but almost have experienced two or three of them at a minimum.

MJD: That's certainly what I felt, and you sort of jump all over the cycle until you don't any longer. It's an apt observation, but when you think about it, it's actually quite obvious. You lose your faith, which is everything, and that is something to grieve. I lost my faith, which led me to becoming quite atheistic, and that is something I'd like to cover in the next session, if you don't mind.

MC: Sounds like a good plan.

---

1. Matthew Korpman is a Yale-trained biblical scholar who wrote the book *Saying No to God*, which posits that it is our biblical mandate to say no to God when ethically appropriate.

THE DEATH OF GOD

Session Five

Michelle Collins: Last time, we ended up talking a lot about early adulthood. But now let's move into your late twenties. I know that you've talked about going through a period of atheism or agnosticism, and I'm of the mind that that is pretty prevalent among people going through the deconstruction process—that it's either a short stay at the very least or it's a place where they end up staying for quite a long time, maybe forever. So, talk a little about that. How was that process for you?

Matthew J. Distefano: You're right. It's common among people who deconstruct, and like we've discussed, there's no formula to this. But it does seem to be common that people get to the question, "Does God even exist?" And a lot of people settle on the answer of, "I don't know," or even "no, absolutely not." And look, I get it. I was there for a while throughout my late twenties, and for me it was sort of uncomfortable but there was also some peace in it because at least there wasn't an asshole-God "up there." So, this may have been something that upset you, but I stick by it: You just have to get to a place where you question the very existence of God. And you might come to a place where you don't think that's the case. Or, you're unsure at the very least. That's what it was for me. I've explained it as riding the uncomfortable fence between atheism and agnosticism. And on some days, I was more atheistic while on others I simply said, "I don't know." To some degree, that is a healthy place to be. I think it strips us of our need for certainty and that is indeed quite healthy. We should hold everything loosely. That's what I believe now. And I think it takes getting to that place for us to realize that.

MC: Right. We both know an individual who believes certainty is one of the basic necessities of life—speaking from a psychological perspective, that is. In other words, that we in fact need a certain amount of certainty. And I think that when you're involved in the religious community, certainty has almost been elevated to that of faith. Like, faith means that you're certain of something, which of course I now contend, and I know you do too, that faith is the exact opposite of certainty. Faith is mystery. And so, we reach this place, like you said, where you crave that certainty. And your comment did upset me because I couldn't imagine, after a whole life of trying to please this idea of God, that maybe he didn't exist. That just seemed too far-fetched for me, and so I ignored that or rejected it more often than not. I rejected it outright. However, I did find that you were right and you end up reaching that place where you're just not sure; and like I said early on, I had a conversation with my daughter a while back where she asked me if I believed in God, and I said, "Today? Yes. That could be different tomorrow." Does it kind of feel that way to you sometimes? Maybe not so much now; but some years back, did it feel that way?

MJD: It did. And like I said, I wavered back and forth between thinking there might be a God and not believing there was. Now, I'm confident that there is something we can call "God." I think the more interesting conversation, however, would then be what is that God like? Any time we talk about God, I think we're actually talking about theology because I think we can only talk about God in terms of an analogy or a pointer. We can never directly talk about God. We can only experience God. So, I am pretty confident that there is a God and I'm pretty confident about what that God is like based on my experiences of life and theologizing and realizing that no matter what I say about God, God is always going to be "other." In other words, my words are only going to point towards God, and I'm okay with that. I'm okay with only being able to point in that direction. Like you said, a lot of Christians aren't. They conflate faith and certainty just like they conflate God and theology. Faith is realizing I can only point at the moon. Faith is realizing when I write out the letters "M-O-O-N," I don't actually think that *is* the moon, if you catch my meaning.

MC: That's a good example. Peter Rollins made a statement one time that impacted me and it's something that I think of all the time. He essentially said, "The minute you begin describing God, you've diminished him."[1] And I really had to think about that but I find it to be true because, like you're saying, we can never fully grasp this idea of God, so at the very best, all we're doing is taking these very futile attempts at some kind of description, which is still only from our limited perspective, experience, and knowledge. But, I'm curious: You went through this period of agnosticism or atheism and now you say that you're fairly confident about your ideas of God, so what shifted? What changed?

MJD: The biggest thing was realizing that everything I believed about God before this time was really just theology. And it was bad theology. So, to paraphrase the oversimplistic phrase that Rob Bell uses:

"I don't believe in that God either."[2] To that end, when I listened to Hitchens or I listened to Dawkins, and they would intellectually destroy apologists on the theistic side, I can now say that I don't believe in the God being argued over because of different ideas about God that I came across in my mid to late twenties and even into my thirties. You see, in our churches, we never talked about the writings of theologians who were "out there"—the heretics and misfits, the Rob Bells or going back further, the C.S. Lewis types. We didn't read George MacDonald. We didn't read the church fathers and mothers like Gregory of Nyssa or even Teresa of Avila. We had Augustine and Calvin and even Luther to some degree, but then MacArthur and Piper and all of them. And so, what *they* said about God *was* God, or so it seemed. Looking back, I realize that it's only bad theology. So, when you come across a God who is unadulterated grace or unadulterated love, or when there is no quid pro quo in God—that you don't change God's mind about you by doing x, y, or z, or even by accepting Jesus as your Lord and savior—you realize that maybe the people who were teaching me otherwise were just as ignorant as anyone out there. You then have to reevaluate the whole thing because when you're watching New Atheists debate folks like William Lane Craig, you realize, for as bright as someone like that is, the whole thing is a strawman. It's putting forth this asinine understanding of God that has nothing to do with direct experience. It's putting forth this bad theology and acting as if it *is* God, and there are plenty of theists who would agree with me there. So, I had to step back and look at it from another angle and see if that angle lined up with my experiences, my encounters with bliss, with love, with mercy, with grace. If it didn't, I could reject it and still say, "Maybe there is a God and maybe God's love and mercy and grace is wider, higher, deeper, and broader than we can ever imagine." And maybe, just maybe, that's the end of the story and it doesn't have to be balanced out with wrath and anger and violence.

MC: I had to laugh the other day while in my garage. There's a bunch of stuff out there from when my daughter was in college where she attended a Baptist university. Peaking up through one of the tops of the boxes was a book by John Piper. It's literally sitting in my garage. I thought how frightening it is to me that she was taught only from that perspective. It wasn't as though they brought in different perspectives and allowed them to evaluate. It was, "This is the truth! This man's perspective is the truth." When you talk about Calvin and Luther and Augustine, I wasn't even taught that. I was brought up believing only the narrow things that were taught in my church. It was always from my pastor's perspective. So, there's a lot of ignorance within the body of Christ that we all just go on what we've been taught. No one examines or explores, and I'll be honest with you, you mentioned Hitchens, and I don't know that debate. I don't know it. And I'm sure there's others that don't know it. So, maybe expand on that a bit. What was the debate?

MJD: Let me clarify something first: I wasn't given Augustine's books or Calvin's books but when I look back, that's what my pastors were running off of—this sort of Augustinian notion of original sin, or doctrines like that. And we weren't even a Calvinist church, but it just goes to show you how many assumptions are made in our churches. I don't even know if my pastors knew that they were preaching Augustinianism when they emphatically were.

MC: Exactly. How many of them had formal educations? Probably not very many of them.

MJD: Right. And you're correct, we don't teach the history of Christian thought. We teach what is so-called biblical doctrine. I was listening to Richard Rohr talk about this on Pete Holmes' podcast.[3] The beautiful thing about his upbringing in the Catholic tradition—and I don't think all Catholics do this, but he certainly did—is you're not taught Christian theology per se; you're taught the development of Christian theology. So, you get all these different perspectives and then it was your job to wrestle with them.

MC: That seems healthy.

MJD: It does! I would have liked to know where the doctrines I was taught were true came from. Where did my beliefs come from? For instance, where did "Left Behind" theology come from? Oh, the 1800s . . . okay, that changes things, doesn't it?

MC: Right. I didn't know that growing up. I just assumed we were all getting taken up in the air at some point and I was to wait for it.

MJD: That's right. Now, as far as the Hitchens debates go; they were the classic debates about the existence of God. So, you have all the different arguments presented. You have the so-called Watchmaker analogy. You have the ontological arguments. You have the teleological arguments. Arguments from Aquinas and others. And then you had debates about the Divine Command Theory, which for some reason theists like Craig would argue in favor of. And this goes back, in a way, even to Plato. *Is it good because God does it or does God do it because it is good?* You know, those sorts of questions. But you'd have these apologists explaining why God is genocidal in the Bible, and why it's okay, and why it's allowable, and Hitchens and others would destroy these arguments because it's simply morally reprehensible when you look at it objectively. But there would be the Christian apologists who were trying to explain away these things, or why they made sense to them and why God should still be God and why God is still considered good, even though, for all intents and purposes, it's not what we would call good. And I had to look at those arguments and admit that they didn't go the way of the theist because I, too, could not square a God who was supposedly the very essence of Love with these things they're saying about God or what God has done throughout history. For me it became clear that if I'm going to be objective and rational and reasonable, then I had to reject that God, which was the only God I knew at the time. Ergo, there was no God for me at that point in my life.

MC: I can identify with that pretty significantly because I'm still kind of in that place. I do find myself, at times, wishing for God and the way I think he should be. But then I chastise myself and say, "That's what *you* think he should be." So, I'm constantly arguing and analyzing, but then again, I'm a very analytical person, so I will argue this to death within myself. But I can't square that either; I can't square why God demands that I forgive my enemies and pray for those who persecute me, yet he is allowed to burn them for eternity. That seems like overkill (no pun intended). So, I'm still squarely in that place where maybe God just doesn't exist and it is what it is. I think what else enters the conversation is your worldview. You have to bring in what you're witnessing happening in the world. How does that square with a God who is supposed to be in control? He's supposedly the go-to for so many people and yet he tends to become a battering ram for many in those circumstances that seem unjust or unfair. I know I've heard you say that before, too, but maybe expand on your worldview at that time and how you handled looking at the world through the eyes of someone who says that there is possibly no God.

MJD: You brought up a couple good points that I'd like to touch on. The first being, how are we supposed to forgive our enemies while God burns his? That, for me, comes down to a theological question and you simply don't have to believe in that theology. The harder one for me is the theodicy question: Why is there so much bad shit going on in the world and where is God right now? It's easier when you don't believe in God because then it's just naturalistic. What we're calling "bad" really isn't bad; it's just life. Things live and then they die.

MC: Right. We no longer have to assign a value to anything. It just is.

MJD: Take COVID-19 for instance. That's just a chemical or biological process, a virus that's just doing what viruses do. It's just "living," if that's what you want to even call it. If you want to take all "meaning" out of the equation, the virus is just trying to find new hosts and it's only "bad" because we value the human being, right? We value sentient beings. In the natural world, it literally doesn't matter to anyone but us. A lion isn't thinking about the ethical killing of a gazelle, so far as we can tell. I'm not saying it's easier to be an atheist; it's just that you don't necessarily have to answer the theodicy question. Shit happens because that's the way it is. On the flipside, though, maybe God's not in control. That's where I'm at now. And that can be a little bit scary, too, or it can be quite motivating in that we have to get off our asses and do stuff. We do have some human agency and there is a valid reason for that. We do have some volition. We do have decisions to make. Now, that doesn't answer the question, "Why do kids get cancer?" or things like that. Those questions are the hardest for me, and even David Bentley Hart says that any atheist worth their weight is going straight to *that* question.[4] It's not even the Hitler argument or anything like that—the better question is the so-called "natural evil." Why does *that* stuff happen? I just throw my hands up and say, "I don't know. Because bad shit happens." I don't really have an answer for that and I'm still quite agnostic. I don't know why God doesn't step in and do something because I would if I could. And maybe that's the point, too. Maybe there's something to the answer that we need to figure this stuff out and do it ourselves. And maybe it takes generations upon generations to do so. Maybe that's a part of human evolution. I have no clue, and I'm okay with that. Healthy agnosticism is something I can affirm. I don't need to be certain about any of this. I still have faith that God is good and while I have questions for God—sometimes it's nothing more than "What the fuck, man?"—I guess I'm good where I'm at.

MC: I think that's one of the most honest prayers I've ever prayed.

MJD: It is. And I'm okay with having that and I think God is okay with me asking that. So, again, I think that is the difference between faith and certainty. I don't need to come up with some wonky apologetic for why God is allowing horrible stuff to happen. I don't need to write that book. I don't need to debate it because I don't know. I have no solid idea why bad stuff goes on.

MC: And that is probably a really big sticking point for those going through the deconstruction process. It is for me. That's the stuff that I will sit and analyze over and over and over and I do come to some short-term conclusions along the way. First of all, I don't believe and will never believe that God is the one that hands out disease as some form of divine punishment. I think that is bat-shit crazy, to be honest. And I don't know why you would want to worship a God that was so arbitrary in his anger.

MJD: I don't know how you can.

MC: I don't know how you can either. I don't know how you ethically or morally can. But I have made the arguments within myself that maybe God is not in control. Maybe God put all of this into motion and while he's not controlling individual aspects, he is available to be the suffering savior alongside us, so to speak. In other words, God suffers along with us. But then again, that is kind of repugnant to me as well because then he's kind of a sissy. Because if you have the ability to fix it and you choose not to just so you can mourn with me, I still have an ethical problem with that. This is what goes on in *my* head.

MJD: Those are the ones I wrestle with, too. I get Moltmann's co-suffering God. I do. Because there is some comfort to that idea. Sometimes, when someone's suffering, all you can do is sit in silence with them.

MC: Yes, because you don't have the ability to fix it for them. But if God is doing that, I have to assume that if he put it all in motion, he should have the ability. And then you'll have the people that say, "Well, that steps on free will." But I find that ironic because I don't find that anywhere—the idea of free will. I may be wrong about that, and I know you've heard this before, but the idea that God doesn't cause hell, we choose it for ourselves, is utter bullshit.

MJD: As I understand things, it's a complete distortion or misunderstanding of free will. It's putting too much onus on the so-called autonomous human, or a faulty definition of free will, as if God couldn't design freedom to be different than what the libertarians say it is. I've heard David Bentley Hart talk about this in many places.[5] We typically think of free will as in the ability to choose between X, Y, or Z, but maybe free will is better understood as only being able to choose that which is good. Put better yet, free will isn't having the ability to choose between different things, it's having the clarity to choose the obvious good, and it is only obvious to those who are actually free. That, I think, is true freedom. You no longer even have a choice because the so-called choice is so damn obvious. Why? Because that's how we're "designed," for lack of a better term. We come from a source that is good and we are moving to a place that is good so maybe freedom is simply doing that which is good. Thinking like this starts to become helpful for me when it comes to the free will discussion, because I really hate the argument you just touched on—as if all these people who argue for us to "freely" choosing hell are philosophers, that they took seriously their philosophy courses, and that they have at minimum a bachelor's degree. I mean, they talk about human volition as if this has not been an argument that has been going on for thousands of years, all the way back to Kant and Ockham and even Plato and Aristotle. We're talking about the eternality of hell and people choosing that? It's rather absurd. One who does that is no freer than someone who shoves their face into a fire in the name of spontaneous autonomy. We would never call that person "free" or even sane. They're enslaved to something. That person needs help.

MC: One of the greatest explanations of that I've come across so far is from Robert Farrar Capon. He presented a scenario in which he said, and I'll paraphrase: *Maybe you are free to choose hell because that's what you choose to experience, but maybe heaven or the kingdom is happening all around you and it's only when you change your mind and realize that you already are a part of this so you then begin to experience it.* That actually made some sense to me as far as why people think that you can choose hell. Maybe that's what they experience. Maybe they're living in a hellish experience right now and so you can imagine that. So, it comes down to my focus, or in other words, you tend to experience what you expect to experience. With regards to hell, then, maybe because they experience something similar now, that's what they expect to be on the other side.

MJD: I think there's some truth to that. I would take it one step back, though, and ask the questions, "What is the mechanism that changes your perspective? Are you picking yourself up by your bootstraps, or is there some sort of change that is done in partnership with the divine?" I would always tend to guess that if it comes down to you changing your perspective and experiencing life in such a way that it's more blissful than hellish, then it's by the grace of God first, which then causes a shift in your experience. That rings true to me. So, on the one hand, I believe in free will to some extent because I feel as if I am free in some way, but still enslaved to biological and chemical processes that I can't simply will away. I can't will away depression. It just is. And while I can shift my experience of it, I'm not a wizard who can snap his fingers and make it disappear entirely. We are, after all, a product of our circumstances and our DNA.

MC: Which is, of course, an extension of our choices, so maybe free will is involved in this after all.

MJD: To some degree, but also, "Am I my brother's keeper?" Yes. There is intergenerational trauma. So, it gets more complex than saying how you just have the freedom to do this or that, to give your heart to the Lord, for instance.

MC: Yes, that's a very simplistic viewpoint. No one is able to live to that level, certainly not for any length of time. If we're talking about a small choice, then maybe you can pull that off. But as you start talking about disease and existential crises and depression and all of these hardcore topics, that doesn't work anymore.

MJD: It didn't for me. And this is the deal: It seemed to work for my friends in church and my pastors, or at least they faked it really well. This is the problem I had. I couldn't fake it. I had these questions, and I heard these stock answers to the point where I thought they weren't even really thinking about it. They were just throwing out these answers willy-nilly as if they satisfied, and they don't.

MC: You also have to remember that you're getting what they present, and not necessarily what they actually think or feel internally. And of course, within Christendom, were taught that we're supposed to project faith and positivity and all these things, and so they go into these conversations from a very "pie-in-the-sky" viewpoint. If I'm honest, that used to piss me off because it would make me feel like an utter failure. I think about that a lot still to this day. I have a very good friend that I went to church with for years who has stage-IV cancer, and he just found out. When I talked to him through Skype, he said he feels like God is not done with him yet and he was very positive about it, and I was thinking how I could not be there if it were me. I would have to be angry for a little bit, and scared, and maybe he is those things but my point is that he's not projecting that. He's projecting a positive and faithful attitude as if God is going to miraculously heal him. But how many millions of times has God *not* miraculously healed, even those that claim belief in him?

MJD: I think both feelings have to be allowed. The problem is that in church you're only allowed to have the "God is in control" or "God is going to heal me" view. You're not allowed to be angry with God. You're not allowed to lament. You're not allowed to be pissed off. That's the problem. You should be able to suffer and be not okay. That should be allowable in the church. See, we have a culture of "fine." And there's nothing wrong with being positive. Take, for instance, that Buddhist monk who lit himself on fire in protest. He must have been suffering in the worst ways and yet while everyone around him is freaking out, he's the calm one. That's one extreme, and it should be okay. But it should also be okay to not be okay.

MC: I agree. And from a psychological perspective, I believe that's healthy. I think we have to deal with the emotions that we suffer with in order to work through them. If we begin to stuff those down, as often is the case within Christianity, we end up psychologically damaged, especially if the healing never comes, or that job never comes, or the child is stillborn regardless of our viewpoint. I vividly remember my sister-in-law having a baby that basically didn't form a skull, so she carried the baby to term and when it was delivered, it died. There was no way around that. And I remember the whole way through, praying, "That child is going to be miraculously healed." But that didn't happen. My kids were devastated. I was devastated and trying to figure out why God would allow that. So, I think it does psychological damage to us if we only look at life from that uber-positive viewpoint. But life just doesn't work that way.

MJD: Could you imagine going into most churches and being really real and raw with where your emotions are at? It wouldn't be okay, which is so opposite of what the church should be. It should be totally safe. It should be safe to have the honest of prayers. If "what the fuck, God?" is all you have, then that's all you have and the church should be there with you in it. But what we typically do in the church is to take those moments—and we all have them—and turn them into gossip: "We all have to pray for Matt because, well, you know, he is backsliding and you should have heard his language, and blah, blah, blah." We are really missing the point when we do this. I just said it but it bears repeating: We should all be okay with not being okay.

MC: Yes, because it's honest. There's no one that is okay all the time. I think we want to project that we are because it makes us feel better to think that others think we have it all together. But it's just not honest. It's not ethically right, in my opinion.

MJD: I'm hoping there's a movement toward vulnerability being seen as a strength rather than a weakness, and there seems to be some of that going on. The church just seems to be lagging behind, like always.

MC: I've heard that the church typically lags behind around 150 years in thought.

MJD: Well, it certainly seems that some of us are living in the 1870s.

MC: Again, it comes back to wanting to present a certain type of image, namely that there's an attractiveness to God because it's still very much about evangelizing to people. And so, if you're trying to sell something, you want to present the best picture you can, even in harsh circumstances. So, I think that tends to be the go-to formula. However, it fails in its attempt to meet people where they are. That's a downfall of much of the church right now. And all of it plays into a sense of grief. It plays into a sense of anger and depression and all of those things we associate with grief because we are struggling to make sense of something that we don't have the ability to make sense of. So, it makes sense that for a period of time; they get to a place where they're not sure they want to believe in God anymore. I feel that way often. If God cannot be any better than what I think I should be, then we're in a big world of hurt. I don't want to serve something that is damaged, if that makes sense.

MJD: It does, and it's okay to be where you're at. That's the big takeaway I'd want for people going through this. It's okay to simply learn how to float where you are. You often have no other choice.

MC: Right. It's not as if you can grab your ball and go home.

MJD: Nope. You're in the middle of the ocean at the moment so you have to just learn how to float.

MC: Yes. And anyone reading this to this point who is looking for an answer is going to be severely disappointed because there is no answer.

MJD: That's the point. There is no formula. We've said this a couple times already. You can outline how you think your deconstruction is going to go. You can think it's going to be linear, but when you look at it, it's just a ball of yarn that's tangled up into a conglomeration of nonsense. Pieces are strewn about, not even connected. And maybe the point is to just put your tangled-up ball of nonsense next to someone else's and do it in community. Do what we're doing. Do what folks are doing online—however you can connect with people, because then you have a sense that you're okay and not alone. And if you're not okay, you can be not okay together.

---

1. As we noted early on, in *How (Not) to Speak of God*, Rollins introduces the idea that we must "embrace the a/theological approach that acknowledges the extent to which our supposed God-talk fails to define who or what God is" (Rollins, *How (Not) to Speak of God*, Introduction).

2. From Rob Bell's "Everything is Spiritual" tour, which you can view at https://www.youtube.com/watch?v=JT09JbaEh_I.

3. https://www.stitcher.com/podcast/puck-soup/you-made-it-weird-with-pete-holmes/e/45844254?autoplay=true.

4. For Hart's answer, see "David Bentley Hart: Atheism's Best Arguments?" which can be found at https://www.youtube.com/watch?v=AQBfoneh97E.

5. See, for instance, Hart's epic masterpiece, *The Experience of God: Being, Consciousness, Bliss*. New Haven: Yale University Press, 2013.

PUTTING THE PIECES BACK TOGETHER

Session Six

Michelle Collins: We've spent a lot of time talking about the history of your belief system and the places in which you began questioning. We've even touched on relationships and how they were affected by all of this, but let's talk a little bit about where you go from there. Of course, another word that's being used a lot right now is "reconstruction." You and I have talked about that, but I don't know if that's how we want to say it. There is, however, something to the idea of putting it back together after you've taken it apart: What stays? What goes? And what affect does that have on you? So, we've talked a little bit about some of the beliefs that you had at the time that you started to question, but how did those change? Where did you go from there?

Matthew J. Distefano: There does seem to be a model of deconstruction and then reconstruction. I find that to be the case for a lot of people but it's not necessarily a universal truth. On the Heretic Happy Hour Podcast, Brad Jersak talked about it as an art restoration project.[1] So, you don't necessarily need to whip out the hammer and knock everything to the ground and then start putting pieces back together. I suppose that's what it looked like for me. I burned it all to the ground and then started over. For some that can be a bit obtuse. It's just one of those things that—call it the grace of God or call it fortunate circumstances—you just start to run into different voices saying different things about God that make you say, "Huh . . . I've never heard that, so let's explore it." And, like we talked about in the last session, you then start to realize the theology you were given your whole life was just that: theology. It wasn't God. And more often than not it's really bad theology. So, it gets you asking new questions when you come up against different thinkers, different mystics, different "enlightened" folks who are saying different things about God that you've never heard but you then feel in your bones that you have to consider. Fortunate for me, I ran into someone locally who I *had* been friends with, who is now my best friend—Michael Machuga—who was asking the same questions and having the same insights and thoughts independently of me. When our lives ran back into each other, we realized that we were having this deconstruction/reconstruction process, or were in the midst of it, enough so that we said, "Hey, we should probably sit down and talk."

MC: One of the things that's interesting about this whole notion of deconstruction—it seems to be a common experience for most people who are self-identifying in the process—is a lack of community, a lack of connection that we kind of take for granted when we're involved in a church or small group setting. I've often referred to those as lazy relationships because they're convenient. But that is something that everyone tends to struggle with—the lack of relationship or communing with other people as they go through this process. So, how did it transpire that you guys sat down and started talking about this? Was it just, "Hey, I'm going through this process; are you going through this process? Let's dish it out." Or, was it just feeling each other out? And then suddenly realizing that you have something valuable in common.

MJD: It was actually much more dramatic than that. I was Facebook friends with Michael's wife, and you know how I am on Facebook—I can be just a little bit vocal and opinionated—so naturally was saying some things that sparked her curiosity. Michael had a dirt-bike accident where he almost died back in 2014, where he went over the handlebars. He's an avid dirt-biker in his own right but had a horrible crash in which he severed his liver and spleen and broke his collarbone. And so, he was laid up, in and out of the hospital for weeks on end, and his wife pointed him to my Facebook and basically said, "Hey, look! Matt's kind of asking and exploring these same questions as you, Michael." So, she told him that we should probably talk. I knew Michael from back in the day. He actually ran sound at my wedding in 2004. We went to the same church. And so, we knew each other well enough. We were friends but not great friends. But then, once it was understood that we were asking the same questions, it was on like Donkey Kong. He was reading Rob Bell's *Love Wins*—the great slippery slope of a book Evangelicals warn people about—and both he and I were reading Tom Talbott and folks like that, so it was clear that we needed to chat about things. These authors and the ideas they presented weren't allowed at our church, but here we were anyway. We started sitting down in the evenings, lighting a fire, having a drink, smoking some herb, and talking. It's funny because in addition to all this, he has colitis and I have celiac and weed really helps us both. It was almost as if the Universe was trying to tell us that we should hang out. I don't know if I actually believe in those sorts of "divine encounters," but I can't help but think if I were still an Evangelical, I would think it was God talking.

MC: It's very serendipitous.

MJD: Yes! So, it just took off from there. It became church. And like you just said, it's *the* thing that people miss about church. They don't necessarily miss the toxic beliefs and things that torment them, but when they "deconstruct," they don't have that community any longer. And even if it's a shallow community in the grand scheme of things, it still feels good. So, this new relationship took the place of church but it was so deep and rich and we had so much in common that we could have three-hour conversations into the night without even blinking an eye.

MC: I had a lot of the same experiences. We even called it that. I started hiking with a friend that previously went to church together with me. She had been gone for a while and we reconnected. Myself, her, and her mother would hike every Sunday. That's what I started doing when I didn't go to church any longer. During our hikes, we would have these very in-depth conversations about God, and at first it was me being very angry and sharing my frustrations and my disillusionment. It was the same with her. Her mother was very agnostic and wasn't interested in Christianity, but she would indulge the conversations, and after a while it became something that we called our church. It was healing. It was cathartic. Not only are you in nature, but you're allowed to express anger and emotion. You could have questions and doubts without someone telling you that you didn't have enough faith.

MJD: Michael and I would hike a lot, too. We've hiked Mt. Lassen,

Mt. Brokeoff, and Sawmill Peak multiple times. And yeah, it becomes church.

MC: It's very healing.

MJD: And it's something that I think would ease the burden of deconstruction. So that's the blessing for me—and I don't like using that word—but it feels like it was a blessing for me to have that. I feel as if it kept me from going insane, and feeling totally alone—alone on this island, all by myself, or drowning in the middle of the sea without so much as even a life raft. When someone comes along who *is* that life raft, you can at least drown together. Really though, you end up realizing that, because of the other person, you're not drowning.

MC: You mentioned that you re-found one another on Facebook, and that's how you and I met. We can say a lot of negative things about social media—there's plenty of negativity out there. But that has been a positive as it pertains to this discussion; in coming across so many people that were questioning and struggling, that were experiencing a loss of communion with church and other believers. Suddenly I felt as if I wasn't alone. There *were* other people out there, who then become face-to-face friends. It definitely has its place if we can just get past all the other stuff. It can be so beneficial to be able to have those connections with other people. And we learn from them while they learn from us. So, like you said, you're drowning but you're not because you're holding one another up.

MJD: Social media is like anything else in that it can be used for good or for ill. It's the same thing as the church. The church, in theory, is a great idea—people coming together, communing, giving what you have to one another in a web-like system. The problem is that we turn it into a clusterfuck. We become hierarchical. We become patriarchal. And it becomes a way to abuse and oppress people in the same way social media can become abusive. We see it happen daily in today's current cultural climate. But, like you said, I can't help but be thankful for it as well, for meeting Michael, for meeting you, and so many relationships that have blossomed because of an initial online meeting.

MC: Absolutely! And again, you bring up a valid point: every one of those examples have the same common denominator. It's people. This is how we function unless we're willing to become very self-reflective and work on ourselves. That's not to say we can't have bad days but when you're seeking out these kinds of relationships and opening yourself up to these kinds of conversations, they're going to be difficult and inspire emotion. And whether that's in a church building or in an online setting, you still have to deal with the human element. You're right, though, church *is* like social media, if you think about it.

MJD: It is. There's a lot of great things about church but a lot of times it turns into an echo chamber. You get around your group or your tribe, you believe these particular things and not those other things, and the minute you shift, you're kicked out of the group, or blocked, or unfriended, or you're excommunicated and perhaps even burnt at the stake, depending on your current historical context.

MC: It all sounds very dramatic but that is accurate. Those are the experiences of many people that have asked any kinds of questions, be it religious in nature or something else entirely. There will always be someone to disagree or tell you that you're wrong. That's just a part of it. So, going back to the relationship you have with Michael and when you started chatting about the things you were learning: What do you think is one of the best things that you've learned from him?

MJD: That all we have is the present moment. He gravitates toward Buddhism and it's funny because I remember the first time we hiked together—we were hiking Sawmill Peak, which became our favorite spot—and I was still deconstructing and still a little fearful of hell and all those things when he told me that Buddhism makes way more sense than Christianity. And I remember being worried about that because in my mind he was already well off the rails, while I was only going off them. It was hard enough to be in an agnostic place but to hear that he had completely "headed East" was, at the time, even more difficult to grasp. It's difficult to shed fear-based ideas even when you think they're gone. They have their tendrils in you even when you think you've gotten rid of them. As we talked more and more and as the months and years went on, however, it started to become clear to me that Buddhism and Christianity should not have a problem with each other. And what he's taught me is that a mystical understanding of each are really just pointers toward the one transcendental truth of God or whatever we want to call it. And yes, they have their individual contexts, but they're really saying the same thing. What he's helped me understand about Buddhism, specifically, is that it's a very direct pointer. It's very much about direct experience. It's very much about here and now because that's truly the only thing we really have. It's a perpetual nowness that helps ground you and become very present. It helps you realize thoughts, though they may be uncomfortable, are neither bad nor good. They simply are, and our problem is being so quick to label things. Labelling is fine in that labels help us talk to one another, but we need not attach ourselves to our labels. Instead, we just use them as pointers. That's all from Michael and it is very helpful for me.

MC: I really like that idea of perpetual nowness. I think it's so easy to be trapped in past events and living from that place, even subconsciously. Or, doing what my former husband calls "future tripping," where we sit and anticipate what we think is going to happen. And I think a lot of that has been built into us in the church, where we're constantly worried about what we've done and then what will come and how we should act in anticipation of that. That causes us to get lost and miss the "now." Recently, someone introduced me to the book *Living Buddha, Living Christ* and it was not a book I would have picked up previously because it would have been too much to handle, but when I read it, all I could think is that I'm Buddhist because it just made so much sense. Oddly enough, it sounded like what Christianity *should* be. What I got from it was that the here and the now, and the idea of mindfulness—centering yourself here and now—is what truly is. This is healthy, from a theological perspective, but also from a mental and emotional and psychological one as well because it disallows the things that may be causing stress to infringe on the moment. So, that's a great lesson that he's taught you.

MJD: I wish Christians understood this. You're right in saying that this is what Christianity should be, but we do have the propensity to look only in the past about either our sins or the event that happened 2,000 years ago on the cross, and how that impacts us not today, but in the afterlife. What happens when we die? And now we've missed this entire thing called now, which, if you think about it, is the only thing we really have. The only thing we really have is right at this moment. And that's not to say that this nowness won't continue on because it will. It is always now, then now, then now, then now, then now, ad infinitum.

MC: It reminds me of our friend Jamal's book, *Living for a Living*. In it, he talks about that a lot: "In this moment, I have everything I need." It doesn't matter if there are bills due or stresses that are sitting out there; in this moment, as I sit here, I have everything that I need. It's so difficult to rest in that knowledge because of those outside pressures. But, even if we are going to look at it from a Christian perspective, that is the way we're supposed to live. Jesus actually spoke of that. It's in the "red letters." So, it's interesting that we have so much propensity to disavow that.

MJD: Especially when it's so helpful in how you live out your faith. It's been super helpful for me and it's a shame people miss it. But I'm reverentially grateful for that insight. And while he's helped me with many other things, that's the one that really sticks out.

MC: I think that's beautiful and again, comes back to the point that it is so beneficial to have someone with which to go through this process because it is so alarmingly isolating. Whether that's real or not, that's the implication for most people. That's how it feels. You feel as if no one has asked the questions you're asking, that you're out there alone and no one understands. You're an apostate. You're a heretic. You're a reprobate. Whatever titles we want to put on it. And we have a tendency to close in on ourselves and not realize that these are actually some pretty common thoughts and questions. So, having that other person to bounce ideas off of without judgment is vital, psychologically and otherwise. It's that act of being able to express yourself without fear of recrimination. To evaluate. To try to understand. That's what we're supposed to do—try to understand with the understanding that we may never fully understand. Maybe this isn't a fair question, and I'll leave it up to you, but what do you think Michael has learned from you?

MJD: Typically, that wouldn't be a fair question, but Michael and I have talked for so long that I feel pretty comfortable answering for him. I think I've done a decent job of getting Michael off his ass in order to do something with the ideas in his head. And he says this in our books—that he wouldn't have written a book without me pushing him. And now we've published multiple projects and did a podcast for a couple years (until he got sick), which he never thought he would do. So, I think that I've done a good job of motivating him while being a safe person to explore his ideas with. If he decided that he didn't want to write a book or start a podcast, there would have been no judgement from me. So, I feel that the safety and reliability and trust that's built over years of having a relationship is a motivator. It's not just that you tell someone to get off their ass and do something, because he's not lazy. He works a 40-hour a week job. It's just about feeling comfortable enough to share these ideas with someone like me, one whom Michael respects, in order to then feel good about sharing them with the broader world. Honestly, he's got great ideas and if they weren't good ideas—you know me—I would push back and tell him.

MC: It's beneficial to have the kind of relationship where that kind of constructive criticism is welcomed, or at least tolerated. We have to make a distinction between that kind of relationship and the kind of relationship we have with a spouse or family member. When it comes to this, there will be different reactions. I wouldn't have some of these conversations with my former husband, for instance, not because I don't care about him or anything like that, but because he was and has been in a different place, if he were even to admit he was in a period of deconstruction at all. It can become a very emotionally charged conversation, and because we lived together, that's probably not the best idea. So, having that person outside of marriage, who you can still have an emotional relationship with, but still feel safe in asking those questions, is beneficial. And I know not everyone is fortunate enough to have those kinds of relationships, but those are the ones that we should cultivate, along with our familial relationships. They are the ones that will help the most, but also get to take a break from because we don't have to live with them. When you live in the same home, it can be difficult.

MJD: Yeah, there was not a lot of emotion to our conversations per se. At the end of the day, it's different if your friend whom you don't live with has a different view than you, than if it's your spouse. With a spouse it can bet a little more awkward.

MC: And that was my point. Those are very different environments and can have a very different outcome, so you have to be careful with that. It is one of the things that many people have experienced within the realm of changing their minds about what they believe; not only did they lose church relationships or friends, but some have lost marriages. Some have lost relationships with children or other family members because there is this need to distance ourselves from what we don't understand in order to protect ourselves. That's a struggle for me to accept. I don't know that I could ever walk away from anyone because of that but it has happened to others. It's definitely a part of the conversation that's difficult, so having that outside perspective is helpful and beneficial. But tell me: How does this look when it does come to talking about all this with a family member, when you start putting back together what you think or believe? How does that look with someone in your family? What was your experience with that?

MJD: Of course, every relationship is going to be different. It depends on the reaction of the spouse or the brother or sister or parent or whomever we are talking about. For me, my spouse was always open to questioning, but not as comfortable with vocalization. So, she was stuck in a place between me and her family, who still to this day, are very hardline conservative fundamentalist Evangelicals. And so, having a new type of relationship definitely takes time. I think it's only recently where she's been more comfortable having a relationship with them from a great distance. Because they're not okay with questioning, or at least they present with being not okay with questioning. I don't think we ever really know what's going on in someone's heart and mind at 9 o'clock at night before they go to bed, when things are quiet and their minds are working overtime. But they present as if it's not okay to question, that it's not okay to have doubt, that it's not okay to be a skeptic, and that they're not okay with you if you are. For her, finding that balance of being agnostic about a lot of things and not being at the same place as me has taken work. And that's okay. But it takes a level of maturity and growth and what Dr. David Schnarch would call differentiation: You stand on your own two feet when it comes to what you believe and what you think, and your intimate relationships are not based on what you think or believe.[2] It's something much deeper.

MC: Unfortunately, those bleed into it occasionally, and that can cause a problem. But it should be based on something deeper than these outside questions or beliefs, because those are always changing. Whether it's as big a change like what we're discussing here—the idea of taking part a belief system—there are still questions and changes that happen. Nobody is robotic. Nobody remains the same. And so, we have to be cautious and guard those relationships, while at the same time allowing for change from one another, which isn't always easy.

MJD: It takes a growing up of sorts. It takes maturity. I remember having a conversation with my brother about all this, and he shed some light on the situation. He said that when you challenge these things, you challenge who people are. And I'm not really doing that because at our core we are not our beliefs. But at the same time, it feels like we are. This is especially true of the Protestant tradition. We are certainly our beliefs, and when you are challenged in that, you are challenged existentially. That's how it's experienced anyway. That helped me understand why it gets so personal when I say what I say. I could come at things from my perspective and have it all be about me and my beliefs and questioning my beliefs, but from their perspective, I'm challenging the very core of who they are. That's where it gets very difficult to have a relationship in the midst of that.

MC: I think I would agree with you that we are not our beliefs, if we are talking about a perfect situation. When I say we are our beliefs, what I'm saying is what your brother is saying, namely that it is a very real experience for people. So, it is challenging to them on a subconscious level. They may not even be aware. Also, we've been taught by Christianity that our identity is wrapped up in our belief in Christ or God and so that's one of the things I've written about, that you begin to lose your sense of self when you begin to question God. So, not only have you deconstructed some of the things that you believe about God, but now you've reached a level of deconstructing yourself because you have to find an identity outside of those beliefs if you're going to question those beliefs, or if you're going to doubt them. And so, this becomes a very real subconscious threat when you bring that into the conversation. It's an immediate trigger, for lack of a better word, in their brain. It's all about emotional self-preservation. It's actually a very fascinating brain science in how that's the job of certain elements in our brain, and so we will push back immediately. That is our experience, and so we are our beliefs in that way of thinking about it. Now, as you said though, in a perfect world we are not our beliefs. We are able to separate and evaluate from an objective standpoint rather than having an emotional reaction, and that's the difference—objectivity vs. an emotional response.

MJD: I can't disagree with you. Our experience is that we are our beliefs, and I totally get that. I just mean, on a deeper level, we are more than our beliefs. But, experientially—phenomenologically—it is as if we are our beliefs, and our beliefs *do* matter. And it does form our identity in the concepts and labels we come up with. This is why Buddhism has been so helpful for me. It's the analogy of crossing a river. You have your boat and your paddles in order to get to the other side. But when you get to the other side, you don't continue to carry your boat and your paddles. And so, the beliefs and the labels take us so far, but then we move on from them, so much so that I believe true Buddhism is transcending the label Buddhist. You don't need the label "Buddhist" any longer. That helped me realize that when people ask me, "Matt, are you a Christian anymore?" I don't have to answer. I don't even think of things like that any longer. I don't need that label. It doesn't mean anything to me. Not only does it carry with it a lot of meaning that I don't associate any longer, but I simply don't find these labels to be helpful.

MC: Well, there is a lot of discussion or study on something that is called "labelling theory," in which, first of all, it has intrinsic value in that it pertains only to our understanding of it. And again, going back to Derrida, his whole thing regarding deconstruction was about unity of text: What are the definitions we're using? In a conversation, we have to agree on that or we may be discussing something completely different. So, using those labels comes with a generalized understanding of what something means, and if we're not specific, and it can cause a lot of problems. Also, as soon as we attach a label to something, especially if it's a label we disagree with, we are able to dismiss them. It's very dehumanizing. And, from that other person's perspective, attaching a label to them, if they accept that label, begins a process in them where they feel like they have to live up to that label. And so, now you have this whole construct at work: Your perception of the label, their perception of the label, and the reality of the label itself. So, labels can be quite problematic, but also necessary. It helps us communicate, but we have to be very careful about how we use them in order to ensure that we are actually listening rather than dismissing because you think you already know what something means. Does that make sense?

MJD: It totally does. And it's why we often hear the phrase from those who have deconstructed, "Well, I'm not *that* type of Christian." Especially here in America, when we hear "Christian" we think conservative Evangelical. And it doesn't take into account Catholicism, Eastern Orthodoxy, Coptic, or any of these other groups. Christian = Evangelical. So, then you have to say, "Well, hold on, I don't hate gay people, I don't support Trump, I don't believe in hell, etc." You have to add on all these attachments in order to even have the conversation.

MC: At which point the response becomes, "So, you're not really a Christian, are you?"

MJD: Yeah, so that's one reason I don't find the term even helpful. It's even become true of the phrase, "follower of Jesus." Everyone says that so even that phrase typically means conservative Evangelical.

MC: I had a conversation with someone, actually not too long ago, where we were talking about this very subject, and they said, "I don't claim that label anymore. I just want to follow Jesus." And I said, "Well, you're going to have to hold on because that, in and of itself, demands more deconstruction. Because whose Jesus are we talking about? Which version of Jesus are we talking about?"

MJD: Exactly.

MC: We are still back to the unity of text question. We have to define the terms in order to have this conversation. So, you're right, there's no point in putting a label on what you are or what you think or what you believe because someone will still misunderstand it, without a doubt.

MJD: Right. You could be talking about Francis of Assisi's Jesus or Mark Driscoll's Jesus and I guaran-damn-tee that they are very different.

MC: And, ironically—or perhaps not so ironically—our idea of Jesus often tends to look a lot like us and what we think.

MJD: Indeed. My Jesus is Mediterranean, smokes weed, and has tattoos. He's also muy guapo.

MC: That's the ego inserting itself into the conversation, which again proves how important it is for us to define what it is we are saying, and that we offer the almighty grace and mercy that we like to talk about to the other person in case we misinterpret, or they misinterpret, that we can still maintain a relationship, rather than demonize or distance ourselves from someone because we misinterpreted a definition or mislabeled something.

MJD: Are you saying that we all need to read Derrida? Because he's very difficult.

MC: He really is. It's like trying to learn mimetic theory from Girard. You might need an intro.

MJD: That's what *From the Blood of Abel* was for. Anyway, perhaps this is a good place to stop. We can pick things back up in the next session.

---

1. You can listen to this episode here: https://heretichappyhour.com /2017/11/07/006-do-we-worship-jesus-or-the-bible/.
2. See Schnarch, David. *Passionate Marriage: Keeping Love and Intimacy Alive in Committed Relationships*. New York: Henry Holt and Company, 1997.

FINAL THOUGHTS AND WORDS OF ADVICE

Session Seven

Michelle Collins: Last time, we mentioned the word "reconstruction," and discussed what we both thought about it as it pertains to the deconstruction process. But is it absolutely necessary to tear something down and then rebuild it? That's the question I want to explore in our final session. Is it absolutely necessary to do something called reconstruction as a part of this process?

Matthew J. Distefano: No, it's not absolutely necessary. It seems like there is a pattern, as we've said, where people burn things down and then rebuild them. I fell into that pattern, not in order to be formulaic, but just because that's what happened. But, again, as Brad Jersak has told me, it can be more like an art restoration project than anything else.

MC: To be fair, I think he was quoting Brian Zahnd.

MJD: Okay, so credit where credit is due. Regardless, the answer to your question depends upon a number of different factors: how indoctrinated you are, what is your personality type, what's your psychology, how much trauma you've gone through, etc. You know, some people don't have traumatic experiences caused by religion, even though they have had the same belief systems as those who are traumatized. For instance, the Gimli to my Legolas, Michael Machuga, grew up with the same belief system as I did—for the most part—but it didn't emotionally and psychologically impact him to the same degree it did for me. There was still fear. There was still not knowing where you're going when you die. But there wasn't the type of trauma that I seemed to have, where you are in a perpetual existential crisis, suffering from recurrent nightmares on the regular.

MC: Part of all this is realizing that how you got into your deconstruction will have big effect on how you *do* the deconstruction. And because my contention is that it follows the cycle of grief, there's different kinds of deconstruction (because there's different kinds of grief). If a loved one, for example, has passed away due to old age, that's a different kind of grief than someone who is violently murdered. My reaction in that grief, then, would be different based on that. So, I think that's what you're talking about. Some people can challenge their beliefs without feeling as though they've been hurt by God or by the church or by other people, while for others, it feels like a betrayal, and there's anger or sadness or bitterness or depression or any number of emotions that go along with it. I had some of the same experiences as you. My deconstruction was not pretty.

MJD: I think it's important to note, as we have throughout this book, that even though we've gone through what people call deconstruction and reconstruction—where you burn shit to the ground and then put pieces back together (to whatever degree that may be)—it doesn't have to look like ours did. In other words, any time someone comes along with a formula, then that's a firetruck-colored red flag. Regarding any of those books out there that are like, "The 12 Steps of Deconstruction," I would be very hesitant to promote those because I don't think you can systematize this sort of thing. And I wouldn't want to import my experiences onto someone else and tell them that this is how it's going to go for them.

MC: Well again, we've mentioned this before, but the idea that anyone who comes along and says, "This is how you deconstruct," or "This is how you reconstruct," has basically set themselves up as an authority on a subject in which they don't have any kind of authority. After all, this is a fairly newly understood process, as well as being so individualistic and subjective, so I hesitate with those kinds of things as well. They actually annoy me and kind of make me angry, because it says that somehow my process is wrong because it doesn't look like their process. It delegitimizes other people's experiences, and that bothers me.

MJD: And that's why we've taken the approach we have in this book. At the end of the day, this is my process and you have chimed in on your process, but it's not *the* process. It's *a* process that is totally subjective. And maybe it will resonate with those reading it, but it will look slightly different for everyone who does, and for everyone who goes through a process that is in this realm of what we call deconstruction or reconstruction.

MC: Right. And more than anything, it feels like we're just trying to provide an atmosphere where people know they're not alone. Regardless of the experience itself, you are not alone in having the experience.

And you're right, while this is not *the* process, it is my process and your process and hopefully others can garner some kind of help from that. Or, even just the feeling that you're not suffering in this by yourself, is sometimes enough. That's my hope anyway.

MJD: That's the big goal. It's about being okay even when you're not okay. We've gone through this sort of thing, we've talked to so many others who have gone through this sort of thing, and it's just a way to sit with the other people. And while we can't know all the millions and millions of people who are going to read this book, this is a way to sit with others who are going through something similar. Hopefully they will think, "These two are going through this. I'm going through this. I'm not losing my mind because I'm going through this. I'm not by myself or some complete outlier on the fringes of society for having gone through this."

MC: Which is how we often feel, by the way.

MJD: Yeah, because we end up on the fringes of our church society, and while it's becoming more prevalent, or at least better understood, it's still the minority experience. At the most, only a handful of people from every church are going through this, or at least vocalizing that they are.

MC: So, what do you say to people who have gone through this process at some point or have observed others going through this process, and are now saying that you have to come to some sort of decision?

MJD: A decision about faith or doctrine?

MC: Faith. God. All of it.

MJD: Well, where I'm at now is that God is much bigger than my decisions, no matter what I decide. And while I critique the Bible a lot, it may come as a surprise to some that I still enjoy it, especially the passage about God's love and mercy being wider, higher, broader, and deeper than we could imagine (Ephesians 3:18). No matter what I say about God, I will get it wrong. I will underplay God's mercy and love. To paraphrase something Bernard Ramm once said, God forgives our theology like he forgives our sin. I wouldn't want to turn that statement into a systematized theology, but I still like it because the point being, all of our theology is going to be wrong in some way. At the end of the day, I have my beliefs, but my beliefs aren't what really form me as a person. And they're important to some degree, but they're not primarily important. To the people who have to have doctrines and things like that, I would caution and say that whatever doctrines you hold to, hold them loosely. If you can see the whites of your knuckles, it's probably not a good sign. You're setting yourself up for a house-of-cards situation.

MC: My contention, of course, is that we do this continually. Now that we've started this process or become aware of this process, it is now something that's going to happen on an ongoing basis. Do you feel as if that's true for you or do you think you've reached a landing point?

MJD: If I could make an analogy, it's sort of like creating a sculpture out of wood. At first you take out the big chisel and knock the huge pieces off, but then you get a little finer and more refined. You get a little more detailed. I'd say that I'm pretty confident in my beliefs. I'm about eighty-five percent of the way home. You can tell what I'm sculpting; it just may not be the most precise work of art that exists in the known universe. That is to say, I'm comfortable whittling away at some more of the wood, but I no longer need my chainsaw. I don't foresee there being some sort of grand deconstruction of what I currently believe.

MC: You feel as if you've done the majority of that kind of work?

MJD: Yeah, and I say that after doing a lot of self-reflection—really stepping back and saying, "Why do I believe what I believe?" As you'll recall, when I was a child, my beliefs were given to me. They were handed to me and I didn't know where they came from. So, that's to formulate a worldview in a childish way, but now as an adult, I've obviously started to think about things more rationally, have had more experiences that I have then been able to base my beliefs on, and so it's a much stronger foundation. So, to be perfectly honest, I feel pretty secure in what I believe, with the understanding that I could be wrong about some stuff and I'm okay with that.

MC: So, no more existential crises?

MJD: No, not to the degree that I used to. I still have fears and anxieties and some depression and all those sorts of things. But not the same types of issues I used to have. For instance, I think it is a rather absurd notion to think of a smiting god who's gonna get me if I get things wrong. I don't say that to diminish the fears that people have about that right now. But for me, it's laughable. It's silly, but I understand why some people are still afraid of that sort of thing.

MC: So, if we could look and say that at some point you probably held some form of minor PTSD over those kinds of ideas, that you've come to a place where that's not a problem now? Or, if it is, it's very few and far between?

MJD: Yeah. I've never been diagnosed with that or anything, and I don't know if I would or not. If I had to guess, however, I did have some sort of form of PTSD because of my toxic beliefs. There was, most assuredly, palpable dread and terror for many years, but I don't feel as if I currently suffer from any sort of religious trauma any longer. And I really feel for those who do, partly because I did experience a lot of that when I was younger and know how bad it sucks. What is it? Religious Trauma Syndrome?

MC: There is something identified as Religious Trauma Syndrome, and it can go by a couple of different names. However, it's not in the diagnostic manual. There's nothing in the DSM-5 that alludes to the idea of any kind of religious abuse. Religion, in the diagnostic manual, is often used as a fix for people who are struggling with mental health issues, not as the source of a mental health issue. Personally, I believe that is something that needs to change, because as this experience has shown us, there is a good amount of trauma that's associated with this deconstruction experience. And the closest thing that we have in the DSM-5 to what most people are experiencing here is complex PTSD, in which you are still living within the cycle of whatever is causing you trauma. Simply put, you can't get away from it. And so, for many who are in this process, that's where they are; they're reliving, or still involved in the processes that cause that mental trauma, or that religious abuse, or the uncertainty that leads them to great bouts of anxiety or depression. It's trauma. So, each and every one of us are dealing with a trauma reaction. To that end, I think it's great when we come through a portion of this and we get to a point where that's not as loud in our ear anymore. I can say that I feel as if I'm on that end of the spectrum now as well. I will, however, say that I have not landed anywhere. I'm still not sure there's a God. Some days I'm comfortable with that and some days I'm not. I'd like to hope there is. I'd like to go back to some of the better things I was taught about God and believe that those are true or accurate, but I can't get past the fact that I was wrong before. Honestly, all of this becomes a great unknown. So, it comes down to the idea of how mentally healthy do you feel at the moment? To me, that's what reconstruction looks like. It's not a set list of anything that you have to do in order to be healthy again. It's every day, evaluating how you feel right now.

MJD: That is poo-pooed in Christianity because "it's not about our feelings." But, at the same time, it of course *is* about how we feel because that is derived by our direct experiences and what else do we have but direct experiences? And yes, feelings can be fleeting. Yes, feelings can be deceiving. However, we cannot just say that we should then shed all feelings. Christians often warn about "the world" and how it tells us to just do what feels good but what's wrong with that? There is this idea in Eastern traditions that God, or, more accurately, concrete reality, is experienced as bliss. It comes from the term Satchitananda, and is, to my mind, the best description of capital-R Reality. So, it makes sense that to experience God is to experience pure bliss. I would go so far as to say that if we have a healthy theology, it should bring about peace and joy and bliss to our lives. So, that should be a measuring stick of "reconstruction." Does it bring peace to my life? Does it bring bliss to my life? Does it bring happiness to my life? Do

I feel grounded? Do I feel a sense of homeostasis? Or, on the flipside, do I feel troubled? Do I feel trauma? Am I feeling a lot of anxiety? All these "feeling" questions should be our measuring stick to what good or bad theology is. Forget what you've been taught about doctrine. Forget what you think the Bible says. What am I experiencing right now? What am I experiencing when I meditate? What do I experience when I'm sitting still and focusing on my breath?

MC: That's what I mean! That is truly what reconstruction means to me. It's about taking the time to absolutely celebrate your humanness. So, I've heard it often, in my Christian tradition, the idea that Jesus came to show us what God is like. And I do agree with that. He came to show us a better representation of God. But he also came to show us how to be fully human, which means that we do have emotions. We were created this way. The canon goes into detail about God being jealous or angry or sad or joyful, so why should we be any different? And so, those are a good measuring stick of where we mentally are right now. Of course, I don't think our emotions should control us in any way, shape, or form, but they should be a barometer of what our mental health looks like at any given moment. So, if I feel that I have deconstructed all of my theology, and yet I still feel miserable, then I'm probably not done.

MJD: Absolutely. And I don't know if we are ever really done. We are always a work in progress. In the Eastern Orthodox tradition, they emphasis a process called theosis, which is essentially the process of being made like Christ. The way I understand it is that we are in a perpetual, ongoing process of being made Christlike. And I like that. Michael Machuga and I were talking about this recently. We were saying that in Christianity, we always say how Jesus was perfect, and to me that gets a little bit abstract—as if he wouldn't have grown had he lived an extra fifty years before he died. Are we saying that he wouldn't have learned *anything*? To me, thinking like this strips Jesus of his humanity.

MC: Yes!

MJD: This is all wrong and should be reversed. It should be like this: the more we live and experience life, the more we grow, and the more we deconstruct and reconstruct. We should always be doing that. If we go back to Derrida's understanding of deconstruction, we are always deconstructing because we are always defining our terms so that we don't talk past one another. And we are always reconstructing based on new experiences, which leads us to having new perspectives on life. We should be catching ourselves saying things like, "Oh, I didn't think of it that way." I should be able to say, "Michelle, I didn't see it that way because I am not a woman. Please help me understand your perspective." You know what I mean? Same goes for white folks listening to Black people. And every combination of we can think of. When we have a perspective like this, we can then approach our life experiences or ancient texts like the Bible and try to see things with fresh eyes. We should always be doing this so that we can always grow in understanding of one another.

MC: I agree, because I do think this whole process is an ongoing cycle. That's how I've come to understand it. As uncomfortable as I am with the term reconstruction, I do believe that there always is that building up process in the midst of tearing down. It's going to be a perpetual thing that allows us to learn and grow as human beings. Like you just said, we're not going to be the same person we are ten years from now. And if we are, there is something wrong, because we should have learned a whole lot in ten years, and all those experiences should have affected us on a visceral or changeable level. There's that saying that states if the you of five years ago doesn't think the you of today is a heretic, then you haven't grown. And I tend to agree with that because we're everchanging.

MJD: I tend to agree with that as far as it goes, because we can get to a place where we stop labelling someone heretical, heterodox, or orthodox. The five-years-ago me would disagree with the today me, but I'm not sure the label heretic would be flung either way. And yet, I've certainly grown.

MC: You're right. That saying is a very dramatic way of putting it. But I say this without any doubts in my mind: the me of five years ago would have a lot of problems with the me of right now. She just would. And that's okay, because the me now knows a whole lot more than she did then. So, this idea that we can check off a list and be done deconstructing and reconstructing seems too simple.

MJD: It seems too simple and it doesn't seem experiential. I think of it like this; imagine a permaculture area or a forest. Things are constantly dying and constantly changing and growing. And that's how this whole process is. Leaves fall off the trees and turn into compost. So, we're always shedding things we thought we knew the whole of. But it's just not the case. I can talk about God's mercy and grace until I'm blue in the face but in five years, I would hopefully say that I've learned more about these things since then. That's just how experience works.

MC: To be honest, this is part of the problem I had in writing my first book. It was taking me so long to experience what I was experiencing that my thoughts were constantly changing. So, I would write something and not very long after, I wouldn't agree with it any longer. It became an accordion action, and I was always trying to catch up with what I actually thought. Now I look at that and say it's healthy. That is what we should be doing. I'm going to go back to a term we used in the last session: Perpetual nowness. I have not been able to stop thinking about that. I really like that term because that's what this process becomes. It becomes an exercise in remaining in the perpetual nowness and understanding that may look different tomorrow or the next day, but it will still be now. Being okay with that process is actually what reconstruction looks like for me. It's all about maintaining your perpetual nowness.

MJD: You really do get to a place where you don't have to label things so quickly. You don't have to judge. The great mystics of all faith traditions talk about things in this way, whether it's Richard Rohr in the Christian tradition or whether it's Rumi in the Muslim tradition or whether it's Thich Nhat Hanh in the Buddhist one. What happens is that you get to this place where what you think doesn't have to be labeled. The thoughts that pop into your head don't have to be judged bad or good. You just are. Jamal Jivanjee has talked about this a lot on the Heretic Happy Hour Podcast. He always likes to emphasize how God reveals himself in the Bible as "I am." What I gather from that is how God is just beingness as such. Likewise, we are to be this "I am" as well because we are made in the image and likeness of God. I love that. It strips us of our need for labels and idols because you just are. You are just present. You are here now.

MC: Which is actually a beautiful expression of self-acceptance. And that's what this process comes down to. In the beginning, we start out this process trying to understand God and what we believe about God, and by the time we come to the so-called end of the process—as if we ever get to an end—it's all about who we are and accepting who that is, and understanding that we really know very little. And so, it becomes a healthier mental framework to be able to say, "I know nothing and I'm okay with that," as opposed to thinking you know everything and constantly living in fear of God.

MJD: Right. And while we can never really say we get to the end of this process, there does seem to be a point where instead of questioning doctrines and beliefs that you have, you start to deconstruct yourself and things you never thought you would question or reevaluate, whether it's what it means to be a human, what it means to be a sexual being, what it means to be a parent, what it means to be the church or the unchurched . . .

MC: All of it.

MJD: All of it. Everything. You get down to the point where you've gone from solely talking about God to what it means to be a human being. And that's very scary for people. It's scary enough to question God but when you question who you are, you get into a pretty heavy identity crisis. But what I want people to understand is that they're not alone and it's okay. To quote a great, wise sage: "The only way out is through.

MC: Who was that guy?

MJD: Just some asshole.

MC: He was absolutely right though. As long of a journey as this has been for me, I'm very, very thankful for it. I don't want to be the person I was seven years ago. I don't want to be that person who constantly lived in fear of God and who was so very doubtful of myself (although I am still this way to some degree).

MJD: Correct me if I'm wrong, but you're more okay with being doubtful of yourself than you were seven years ago.

MC: Yeah. I'm doubtful of myself in terms of being capable of doing things, but I'm much more secure about who I am as a person. And I do count that as growth, because we come from a place where we are very distant with ourselves and get to a place where we become intimately aware of ourselves. That goes back to being in the perpetual now, or being mindful. And I know those are terms that cause Christians to recoil because they think it's very new age sounding, but those are helpful terms in how we accept ourselves. Mindfulness is mentally healthy and should be a part of our process. But you can't fake it. You can't force yourself there. I think that's purely experiential and you get there when you get there.

MJD: Yeah.

MC: And another thing. As we get to the end of this, I don't want people to feel as if there is any sort of timeline to all this. Good God, if someone told me that this process would last seven years (thus far), I probably would have had a nervous breakdown. But now I look back and think that's seven years of learning and growing. Those are important years, maybe even the most important years in the grand scheme of it all.

MJD: I've come to the place where the truths of the universe all seem paradoxical. For instance, as similar as our stories are, as many things that we can check off a list in terms of what we deconstructed, it's all unique to the individual at the same time. So, it's almost as if there is an objective path that we all go on, but we all experience it subjectively. And it only somewhat bleeds together.

MC: Right. Even if we have experiences that are similar, we will have experienced them differently. We're all wearing different colored glasses, if you will.

MJD: I always laugh at people who frown upon the subjective experiences of others as if they have objective ones. They need to realize that even if there are objective truths of the universe, we can only approach them subjectively. There doesn't seem to be a workaround with that, nor do I think there should be. I think we have to accept that subjective experience belongs.

MC: Absolutely. And that brings up one final thing that I've had to learn along the way. I used to think that my problem was that I just didn't know enough theology, and so I started reading everything I could until I didn't have the mental or even emotional bandwidth any longer. And I found out and realized that it takes both the education and the experiences to get anywhere. You should, on the one hand, have an educational foundation but even that is going to colored with your subjective experiences.

MJD: And all we can do as people who have done this hard work is to be a sounding board and sit with people and let them vent their frustrations. Hopefully books like this one help, because that's the goal.

MC: If we could go so far as to say that when you started the deconstruction process that you weren't mentally healthy, would you say that you are mentally healthy now?

MJD: I feel as if I am. I do. I have some anxiety, but I think those are general anxieties that human beings have. And I've tried to get to the place where I'm not labelling even anxiety as good or bad. I'd rather just be at a place where I acknowledge that the chemicals are working a little differently and I just have to deal with it as best I can. It's a part of being human. But when I do feel those uncomfortable feelings, it always helps to come back to the present moment. What can I do right now to experience the world in a more positive way?

MC: That is very helpful. I try to remove the emotion of the anxiety and just observe it. That is advice someone once gave me: Don't feel the emotion, observe it. And you said this earlier, but you don't attach a positive or negative label to it, it's just something to understand. I think that is very helpful in this process. Some days it's all going to feel a little overwhelming, but instead of getting mired down in that feeling, observe why. Observe what's happening and allow yourself to learn and grow from it instead of being overwhelmed by it.

MJD: I have to be honest with you, Michelle. You might be a Buddhist.

MC: That's putting a label on it and I'm not going to do that.

MJD: Ah, spoken like a true Buddhist.

MC: Well, the me of seven years ago would be horrified by that but the me now is okay with it.

MJD: Then, like you said, you've reconstructed something worth reconstructing. Indeed, you've even learned to float.

OUT OF THE CLOSET

Bonus Session

Michelle Collins: Throughout these sessions, we've talked a little bit about the subject of sex, but we did it from the perspective of a teenage boy—coming into an understanding of who you are, growing into your sexuality, etc. But let's revisit that subject matter because I think that that's one thing that typically comes back up for a lot of people as they're deconstructing their belief systems. It tends to call into questions things we previously believed, especially with regards to the purity culture and what we believe about homosexuality. After we start deconstructing, many of us start to go back over these issues. As an adult now, has that been your experience? Have you reexamined those ideals?

Matthew J. Distefano: It certainly has. Recently, I acknowledged the fact that I'm bisexual. And look, it's one of those things that when you acknowledge it, you may think it's something new, but when you look back on your life and you look back on the development of your sexuality—beginning as a teenager—you realize it's what you've always been. When you grow up in any sort of puritanical culture, any Evangelical culture, one that says how anything but heteronormative stems from your depraved nature or Satan trying to bring you down, it takes a long time to process through that and to unpack things. We touched on this earlier, but this is one of those issues that you don't know you're going to deconstruct when you first jump into these waters.

MC: So much of this is the unknown. It all just sort of springs up and presents itself to you. I grew up with very "traditional" ideas about sex, but I also came from a background of a lot of sexual abuse, so my thoughts about sex were warped from the beginning. That is something I'm having to reconcile now as I'm deconstructing what I believe about life, about God, and about my beliefs in Christianity. And so, there's a lot of preconceived ideas that we come with that are directly derived from that background. When you were younger, was this something that ever presented itself to where you evaluated it at all? Or did this all start when you became an adult?

MJD: I evaluated it, but it was always harped on us, as you know, that heterosexual is the way God made us. Hetero was the default setting, if you will. So, any feelings or desires that aren't heteronormative get pushed away and shoved down as far as possible because A) you're going to lose your community if you're anything but straight, and B) you're going to lose your salvation. The LGBTQ+ community has witnessed this. You have stories of countless youth being excommunicated from their churches and families and so you become trapped by the fear of being included among these stories. Because of this, you never admit it to yourself, let alone your community.

MC: Like I just said, there's a lot of preconceived notions about our sexuality, especially when it comes to this subject. What I mean is that it's one thing for someone to come out and say, "I'm gay." But there's perhaps a bit of confusion as it pertains to bisexuality. I'm sure some people have this idea that you just haven't made a decision yet. That's kind of an ignorant viewpoint but that's because we have those norms that we've been raised with. So, when you started evaluating that for yourself, was that something you wrestled with? Did you think that you had to make some sort of decision: gay or straight?

MJD: There might have been a little bit of that. I'm not going to say that I was *never* a binary thinking type of person—we all are, to some degree—but that was never something that I felt I had to choose between. My experiences dictated that there didn't have to be a choice. Some guys were cute. Some girls were cute. And that was that. When people say that if you have certain feelings, you have to choose between women and men, it's nothing more than a case of them speaking from a place of ignorance. They aren't letting their direct experiences dictate their epistemology. They don't know what I'm experiencing. On the flipside, there was pressure to choose to be with a woman—and I don't say this as if I'm unhappy to have chosen a woman—that came from the heteronormative church culture. There were no two ways about how they saw things. You were going to be with a woman.

MC: But only after you were married! You have to keep to the rules.

MJD: Absolutely. There are more rules than "thou shalt be hetero." There are other stipulations. But again, I'm not unhappy that I married a woman; it also doesn't mean I'm *not* bisexual. So, to anyone who says, "you married a woman so now you're straight," I'll just say this: you've now attempted to erase me. Or, if people say that I'm confused, then they're not acknowledging my direct experiences. I know this is a buzzword of a pejorative, but they're almost Gnostic. That is, they must have some special knowledge or insight in order to interpret my life for me.

MC: Well, that comes back to people viewing life through their own lenses, their own experiences, and their own comfort levels. I was recently having a discussion with someone about this the other day, and they asked a two-part question that I'll ask you here: What has been the response from the people you told prior to going public, and what was the response from your wife?

MJD: The reaction from what I'm calling my "concentric rings of trust" has been super supportive and positive. I've been intentional about whom I've told, so I kind of knew what the response would be, based on the trust I have for these people. There have been questions, for sure, but they've been respectful inquiries. There have not been any "gotcha" questions. The public response has been more of a mixed bag. Most people have been supportive, but a lot of people have been really inappropriate—from telling me that it's not proper for a bisexual person in a monogamous relationship to "come out," to asking questions about how many men I've slept with, to accusing my wife of withholding intimacy, which in turn drove me to pursue "homosexual intimacy." The worst of all this came from my wife's father, who, in a voicemail to her, accused me of having multiple sexual partners and saying he would never support me. That hurt. A lot. But with regards to my wife, things have been positive and healthy. We've had a lot of long conversations about what all this means, but she's understood that talking to her this late into our marriage—we've been married for seventeen years—is not a result of me hiding anything from her. She understands that for me, this has been a relatively recent acknowledgement of something that's always been there. It takes a long time to put words to what this is. It takes a while to formulate how to articulate something as complex as human sexuality, especially when you don't fall on the far side of the spectrum. There *have* been some things that have bubbled up from the depths of her Evangelical upbringing—"is this just a slippery slope toward coming out as gay?" Questions like this. But she's been able to recognize that that's not how she really feels. That's just some of the church programming—and I use that word intentionally—we both went through.

MC: I can see that. A lot of questions like that come from a place of insecurity. It is big news, and it does impact the person receiving that news—strongly, I would imagine. During a portion of the conversation about bisexuality I was having the other day, the person I was talking to made a comment that goes along with something you just said. They basically told me that "if they get married, that settles the issue then." I asked, "It settles what issue? Are you saying that that resolves any kind of confusion? And that when people finally choose someone, that confusion suddenly goes away?" I went on: "That's not what this is about; this is about something else." Correct me if I'm wrong, but acknowledging that you're bisexual, even though you've been married to a woman for seventeen years, is simply just accepting a part of you that has always been there. It's not about saying, "Hey, I need to express this sexually in the here and now, but that this is simply a piece of who I am."

MJD: That's exactly right. Again, like we've harped on throughout the whole book, this is my experience. Other people might have different experiences. Other people, once they acknowledge their bisexuality, might need to go try things out. And that's their experience, but it's not my experience. I don't want to be with a man, just like I don't want to be with any women besides my wife. It's not really something that I think about. It's not something I want to pursue. However, that doesn't make me *not* bisexual; just like being married doesn't make straight people *not* hetero. Once people get married, they're still attracted to other people. If they say they aren't, they are lying. But admitting this doesn't mean you want to be with them in any sexual or romantic way.

MC: All this brings us back to something you mentioned a little while ago. You said how we all think in binary terms to some degree, and it's because we need a level of black and white certainty instead of recognizing that there's often a middle ground that's more in the gray. Life, though, typically exists in that uncertainty. Part of what's going on for folks who are uncomfortable with this is that they come from a binary worldview, where they've been taught right and wrong. They then have to identify each and every thing that comes their way as right or wrong as opposed as just accepting and realizing that none of this really makes a difference in the day to day.

MJD: That's basically why I'm coming out at this point. It's not something that's going to change my day to day with my wife; it's not going to change our marriage. The only way it's going to change it is in subtle ways, with me being comfortable with who I am. Whenever we do that in life, we're just better people. We're typically happier people. We're more comfortable in our own skin.

MC: Now, I do have a question: Have you discussed this with your daughter, and if you did, how did you go about it?

MJD: I'm glad you brought that up. While she doesn't yet like to think about what humans do with their body parts, she does understand what it means to be gay and what it means to be straight. She will be going into sixth grade next year, so we've had the sex talk with her already. When you raise your kids to be accepting of people, it's not an issue. I'm pretty confident that if she ends up being a part of the LGBTQ+ community, she won't dread telling us. When my wife and I explained that I'm bisexual, she said, "Okay, why are you telling me this?" Not that she doesn't care about me, but just that it's such a non-issue for unindoctrinated kids.

MC: Things are shifting more that way for a lot of people, though I wouldn't say universally because I think there's still pockets of places where it's still very much frowned upon. But a lot of people are raising their children with that understanding, and so it has almost become a "whatever" kind of moment for many people. It seems that is a huge step forward for humanity, especially considering how many people have had damage done to them when they came out. In fact, I did an interview with a gentleman recently who was incredibly damaged when his mother accused him of being gay at four years old. What can a four-year old do that possibly perpetrates that? And so, raising our children with the understanding that sexuality is healthy and normal actually creates that environment that makes it feel safe for them to express that in whatever way they are going to choose to express that. So, that is something to be celebrated.

MJD: Yeah. A lot of people complain about younger generations, but we are actually improving in a lot of ways, and we're setting up the younger generations who will hopefully set up future generations to be better. I'm not saying my parents' generation is horrible, but I was way more nervous to talk to my parents about this than to talk to my daughter. So, in a lot of ways, our roll as parents is to not pass on the trauma that was passed onto us. We know that there is intergenerational trauma and for me, the buck stops here. I'm going to do as much as I can to not pass on the trauma from my father, who we already established was a deadbeat dad. You know, I recall even my mom telling me how he once said if his sons were ever gay, he would disown them. Apparently, he missed his calling as a fortune teller because for him, I'm sure bi is close enough.

MC: Or he was just a deadbeat dad.

MJD: And an asshole.

MC: So, I asked about the reaction of the public and your wife, but what were your parents' reaction when you told them?

MJD: It's interesting because I don't know how affirming they are. Until they moved out of the area, they still attended the same church I grew up in, which by no means is an affirming church. I would say my mom leans more liberal than my stepdad but is still fairly conservative (at least compared to me). But they were both really supportive. My mom said she was surprised but has been one hundred percent accepting. It's funny because other people I've told said they weren't surprised at all. I'm not sure what that means, but I find it interesting. Of course, this support probably wouldn't quite be there if I were in an open relationship. That would have been a different conversation and perhaps had a different outcome.

MC: So, you are going to make it clear right now before anyone suggests it: You and your wife are not polyamorous?

MJD: No, we are not. I'm affirming of those who are, but it's not our bag. Honestly, though, I'm to the point in my life where I don't necessarily care if people accept me or not. I'm thirty-nine years old, been married for seventeen years, and I've got to live my life. Luckily, it's seeming like I don't have to worry about that with my parents though. They've never been judgmental. I would say that they're better than the theology of the church they've attended. I've often said that a lot of us are better than the theology we hold to because it's often the theology that prevents us from being who we really are. I still think that, for the most part, people are better than what they believe.

MC: One on one, that's probably true. It's when people get in a group setting when they feel that mimetic pull to have to belong. Then they tend to be more vocal in opposition. Face to face, people tend to be a little more understanding because it's personalized. It's not just a generalized idea anymore; it's a person standing before them.

MJD: Right. That's a part of contact hypothesis. If people have bigotry or hatred towards another group of people, whether racial, religious, or gender and sexual minorities, then arguments aren't going to change their minds. It's befriending someone. It's having a kid come out as gay. It's one of those situations where it becomes personal. Now they have to evaluate things on a personal level.

MC: We all have this idea about how we would handle something but it's not until we are actually confronted with it that we know for certain what our reaction will be. So, that's a great point and something people need to consider, although I'm not sure we can convince people that they need to consider it. It's hard to get people to listen, with empathy, when people come to us with something like this, because our propensity is to be reactionary. It's kind of hard-wired in our amygdala.

MJD: Maybe we can at least learn to react less, then step back and process things, and then, finally, start to evaluate what's going on. That would be a step in the right direction.

MC: So, the initial public announcement for you was done on the Heretic Happy Hour; how did you handle that? Did you just drop a bomb, or did you have a lengthy discussion about it?

MJD: It was for the 100th episode, so it was a bit of a special show. We tackled a bunch of random questions that were fun to banter back and forth on, but then for the last question, we set it up to where I was the only one who answered. The question was, "What's one thing about yourself that no one knows?" From there, we talked for about thirty minutes and they asked certain questions that they themselves were curious about, but also questions we all thought I might face after the podcast episode dropped. You know—devil's advocate questions. That way, I would have a resource to give people instead of having to personally answer the hundreds of questions that would inevitably come my way. Honestly, that was a great idea because after coming out and facing the nonsense I faced, I no longer have the emotional bandwidth to answer everything from everyone.

MC: Well, the expectation is that if you put something out on social media, then you must engage with everyone who makes an objection. But the reality is that you absolutely don't have to do that. So, setting yourself up to be protected with something like this was probably a smart thing to do, as well as a healthy thing to do. As we wrap up, then, is there anything else you want to add?

MJD: Not really. I would just reemphasize that, like the deconstruction process, this is my experience. Someone who is gay, lesbian, trans, or otherwise, could hear my story and say, "While I resonate with some of that, I don't necessarily resonate with other things because my story is different." Just like each of our theological deconstruction stories, things look similar in some ways, but in many ways they're different. So again, this is just me telling my story, and if it resonates with folks, then that's great. We can stand in solidarity. We can have some commonalities.

MC: Well put. Personally, none of this makes me think any differently of you. I love you no matter what. This just gives me a more complete picture of who you are.

MJD: I love you, too and, appreciate everything about you. Cheers. It's been fun! We'll have to do it again sometime.

BIBLIOGRAPHY

American Psychiatric Association. "Obsessive-Compulsive and Related Disorders." In *Diagnostic and Statistical Manual of Mental Disorders*. 5th edition. Washington, DC, 2013.

_____. "Trauma and Stressor-Related Disorders." In *Diagnostic and Statistical Manual of Mental Disorders*. 5th edition. Washington, DC, 2013.

Ray, W.J. *Abnormal Psychology*. 2nd Edition. Thousand Oaks: Sage, 2018.

Rohr, Richard. *Falling Upward: A Spirituality for the Two Halves of Life*. San Francisco: Jossey-Bass, 2011.

Rollins, Peter. *How (Not) to Speak of God*. Brewster: Paraclete, 2018.

Schnarch, David. *Passionate Marriage: Keeping Love and Intimacy Alive in Committed Relationships*. New York: Henry Holt and Company, 1997.

For more information about Matthew J. Distefano,
or to contact him for speaking engagements,
please visit www.AllSetFree.com

For more information about Michelle Collins,
or to contact her for speaking engagements,
please visit https://www.facebook.com/michelle.collins.9843.

Many voices. One message.

Quoir is a boutique publisher
with a singular message: *Christ is all*.
Venture beyond your boundaries to discover Christ
in ways you never thought possible.

For more information, please visit
www.quoir.com

Lightning Source UK Ltd.
Milton Keynes UK
UKHW020705130922
408795UK00009B/456